Essential
Antwerp

by Marc Willems

Publicist Marc Willems has written for
various newspapers and magazines
and has worked as a researcher for
television programmes. He lives and
works in Antwerp.

Above: *Brabo Fountain*

AA Publishing

Above: *Antwerp is a city of fashion*

Front cover: *Groenplaats; contestants play waterborne polo; statue of Rubens on Groenplaats*
Back cover: *a colourful display of Belgian beers*

Author: Marc Willems
Translated from the Dutch by: Mary Boorman
© 2000 Kosmos-Z&K Uitgevers B.V., Utrecht
Typesetting: Studio Imago,
Jacqueline Bronsema, Amersfoort
© Automobile Association Developments Limited 2000
© Maps: Bert Stamkot, Cartografisch Bureau MAP,
Amsterdam
First edition

English language edition produced for AA Publishing by:
g-and-w PUBLISHING, Oxfordshire, UK

A CIP catalogue record for this book is available from the
British Library
ISBN 0 7495 3191 6

Kosmos-Z&K publishers make every effort to ensure that
their travel guides are as up-to-date as possible.
Circumstances, however, are very changeable. Opening
times and prices change, and roads are built or closed.
Therefore, Kosmos-Z&K publishers do not accept liability for
any incorrect or obsolete information. Assessments of
attractions, hotels, restaurants and so forth are based upon
the author's own experience and, therefore, descriptions
given in this guide necessarily contain an element of
subjective opinion which may not reflect the publisher's
opinion or dictate a reader's own experience on another
occasion.

We have tried to ensure accuracy in this guide, but
things do change and we would be grateful if readers
would advise us of any inaccuracies they may encounter.

English language edition published by AA Publishing, a
trading name of Automobile Association Developments
Limited, whose registered office is Norfolk House,
Priestley Road, Basingstoke, Hampshire, RG24 9NY.
Registered number 1878835.

Printed and bound in Italy by Printer Trento srl

Find out more about AA Publishing and the wide range of services the AA provides by visiting our web site at www.theAA.com

Contents

About this Book

KEY TO SYMBOLS

➕ map reference to the maps found in the What to See section

✉ address or location

☎ telephone number

🕐 opening times

🍴 restaurant or café on premises or near by

Ⓜ nearest underground train station

🚌 nearest bus/tram route

🚃 nearest overground train station

⛴ ferry crossings and boat excursions

✈ travel by air

ℹ tourist information

♿ facilities for visitors with disabilities

✋ admission charge

↔ other places of interest near by

❓ other practical information

➤ indicates the page where you will find a fuller description

Essential *Antwerp* is divided into five sections to cover the most important aspects of your visit to Antwerp.

Viewing Antwerp pages 5–14
An introduction to Antwerp by the author
Antwerp's Features
Essence of Antwerp
The Shaping of Antwerp
Peace and Quiet
Antwerp's Famous

Top Ten pages 15–26
The author's choice of the Top Ten places to see in Antwerp, listed in alphabetical order, each with practical information.

What to See pages 27–90
The four main areas of Antwerp, each with its own brief introduction and an alphabetical listing of the main attractions.
Practical information
Snippets of 'Did you know…' information
5 suggested walks
4 suggested drives
2 features

Where To… pages 91–116
Detailed listings of the best places to eat, stay, shop, take the children and be entertained.

Practical Matters pages 117–24
A highly visual section containing essential travel information.

Maps
All map references are to the individual maps found in the What to See section of this guide.
For example, the Centraal Station has the reference ➕ 31C3 – indicating the page on which the map is located and the grid square in which the Centraal Station is to be found. A list of the maps that have been used in this travel guide can be found in the index.

Prices
Where appropriate, an indication of the cost of an establishment is given by **£** signs:
£££ denotes higher prices, **££** denotes average prices, while **£** denotes lower charges.

Star Ratings
Most of the places described in this book have been given a separate rating:

✪✪✪ Do not miss
✪✪ Highly recommended
✪ Worth seeing

Viewing
Antwerp

Above: *view of Antwerp from the left bank*
Right: *a mime artist on the Meir*

The Author's Antwerp

Antwerp has Napoleon to Thank for its International Seaport
It was the French emperor who began developing Antwerp as an international port. Napoleon was embroiled in a war with England and wanted to equip the harbour for his fleet 'like a gun pointing at the heart of England'. Initially Antwerp did not derive much economic benefit from its infrastructure, because the English set up a maritime blockade. After the defeat of Napoleon nothing stood in the way of the revival of the port.

Antwerpen (Antwerp) owes everything, good or ill, to her port and that also ensures the unique character of her people. For centuries the Schelde (Scheldt) gave the inhabitants of Antwerp a window on the world unlike the rest of Vlaanderen (Flanders). To the locals, known as *sinjoren*, Antwerp is therefore *the* city, and they are inordinately proud of it.

Antwerp keeps on reinventing itself. The 15th century was the Golden Age when the city was the economic centre of the world. The Stock Exchange in London was modelled on the old Beurs in Antwerp. However, religious disputes almost led to Antwerp's ruin. When the South Netherlands broke away from Catholic Spain the Scheldt, Antwerp's vital artery, was sealed off. In addition the majority of the city's economic and cultural elite fled to the Protestant Netherlands because they were afraid of persecution.

It was not, however, the end of the city on the Scheldt. The Spanish court pumped wealth into the cultural flowering of the frontier fortress city, enabling painters such as Pieter Paul Rubens, Jacob Jordaens and Antoon (Anthony) van Dyck to develop their art to great heights. The whole city profited from this growth. Since then Antwerp has experienced a number of ups and downs: repeated closure of the Scheldt, economic blockades under Napoleon, German V-bombs during World War II – but the city has always been able to turn a disaster into an advantage. That is probably typical of a city located on a tidal river.

The port is Antwerp's commercial artery

Antwerp's Features

Facts and figures

Greater Antwerp occupies 20,373 hectares and has a population of 452,121.

There are 146,051 telephone connections and 178,769 cable TV connections – apparently people in Antwerp prefer watching TV to making telephone calls.

The annual consumption of drinking water in the city is 114,524,594 cubic metres.

The power company supplies 226,805 customers who use 975,536 million megawatt hours of low voltage and 960110 million megawatt hours of high voltage electricity annually. Antwerp produces 227,400 tonnes of waste per year.

More Figures

Antwerp has 50 hotels, 2 campsites and 5 youth hostels. These provide a total of 1,053,385 overnight stays. The city boasts 600 restaurants and 1,800 cafés. If you want to have a beer in a different bar every night it will take you nearly five years to visit them all. There are 26 different sites for markets so you would need to do your weekly shopping at the same market just twice a year.

Antwerp's 50 hotels, include the prestigious Astrid Park Plaza Hotel on the Koningin Astridplein

Each year bus passengers in Antwerp make 17,877,845 journeys, a total of 70,130,367 kilometres. The tram is, if possible, even more popular: 37,316,165 journeys covering a distance of 7,255,075 kilometres. The people of Antwerp, young and old, not including the visitors, take a tram on average every four days.

Antwerp has a road network of 1,185 kilometres. As in other large cities this is not enough to prevent a build up of tailbacks during the morning and evening rush hours. There are ten tunnels in Antwerp, under the Scheldt or other roads or railways. These tunnels in particular cause bottlenecks.

As well as 600 restaurants and 1,800 cafés Antwerp has 25 theatres and three large cinema complexes, which are visited on 2,703,000 occasions annually. There are six concert halls and 35 museums.

If you are looking for green spaces in Antwerp there are 25 parks, 6 arboreta, 12 recreation areas and 17 woods and nature reserves.

Essence of Antwerp

Locals and tourists alike love to relax at the pavement cafés

Antwerp is a delightful city with a historic character and an international outlook. Many monuments have survived remarkably intact in spite of the wars and disasters that have affected the city in the past, and Antwerp also has that past to thank for a rich heritage of art treasures. But this city is also a wonderful place for shopping and window-shopping: from the large designer shops on the Meir to the smallest second-hand and curiosity shops in Antwerpen-Zuid (South Antwerp). Eating and drinking are part of Antwerp life and day or night you can easily try out one of the thousand or more bars in Antwerp, or enjoy a first-class meal in one of the many restaurants.

The Gothic Cathedral of Our Lady in Handschoenmarkt

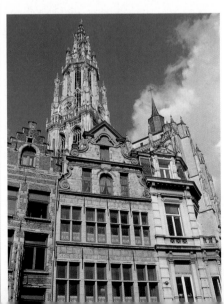

THE **10** ESSENTIALS

*If you have only a short time to visit Antwerp
and would like to attempt a really complete
picture of the city, here are the essentials:*

It is pleasant to walk
along the quays by
the Scheldt

- **Visit the Steen**
(➤ 25), the old citadel
around which Antwerp
was built.
- **Wander along the
quays beside the
Scheldt**. Get a breath of
fresh air and put a coin in a
telescope for a view of the
left bank.
- **Take a look in the
Gothic Cathedral** (➤ 21)
on the Groenplaats (➤ 42)
and absorb the impressive
splendour.
- **Drink a *bolleke Koninck*
at a pavement café on
the Grote Markt** (➤ 16)
looking across to the Brabo
Fountain, in honour of the
Roman soldier who made
the Scheldt toll-free.
- **Go shopping on the
Meir** and move on to
the attractive small shops
near the Bourlaschouw-
burg (➤ 33), or potter
through the antique
shops in Kloosterstraat
(➤ 50).

- **Take a peep in the
Diamondland Showroom**
(➤ 20) and get advice on
buying a gem.
- **Visit Antwerp Zoo**
(➤ 26), unique for its
buildings but even more
celebrated for the animals
you can see there.
- **Be photographed on
the steps of Centraal
Station** (➤ 19), a
masterpiece of
architecture and
atmosphere.
- **Take a look in the
Rubenshuis** (➤ 23),
where you can see
how the artist lived,
and can also admire
some of his beautiful
works.
- **On Sunday morning go
to the Vogelenmarkt**
(➤ 68), submerge
yourself in the hustle
and bustle, or let the
smooth-tongued stall
holders of Antwerp
persuade you to buy.

Antwerp, diamond city

The Shaping of Antwerp

Engraving of Christopher Plantin

AD 100–300
Excavations show that people were already living on the bend of the Scheldt during the Gallo-Roman era. Antwerp grew around two settlements: Aanwerp from which it was to take its name, and Caloes, 500m farther south.

645
The date of the oldest mention of the Aanwerp settlement and the associated fortification (in *The Life of Saint Eligius*).

836
The Normans plunder the settlement and burn it to the ground. The inhabitants then build a wall of earth and timber round it for protection. Traces of this fortification can still be seen in the Steen (► 25).

1133
Foundation of St Michielsabdij (St Michael's Abbey) at Caloes by St Norbertus. This becomes the second centre of power around which the city developed.

1200–25
The earth and timber wall is replaced by a thick stone wall. The river forms the boundary between the German Empire and the French Kingdom. Antwerp is the furthest outpost of the German Empire.

1353
Merchants congregate in the house called 'De Borze'. Historians regard this as the peak of the first economic flowering of Antwerp. Antwerp is the most important trade and financial centre in Western Europe, especially as a port and wool market.

1356
Antwerp is annexed to the Province of Flanders and loses some privileges, mainly to Brugge (Bruges). Fifty years later the political and economic tide turns and Antwerp enters its 'Golden Age'.

1555
Christopher Plantin founds his printing house in the Kammen-straat. He associates with intellectuals such as Justus Lipsius, Gerard Mercator and Goropius Becanus. Antwerp experiences a period of intellectual and artistic growth.

1566
The iconoclasts rage through Antwerp, breaking images and causing great destruction.

1585
Antwerp chooses the side of the Protestant Netherlands in the conflict with Catholic Spain but in 1585 the Duke of Parma, Alessandro Farnese, recaptures the city for the Spanish king. The consequences are disastrous for Antwerp. In four years the population is almost halved, from 80,000 to 42,000. The Dutch close off open access to the Scheldt from the sea and virtually kill Antwerp economically. The most prominent intellectuals and merchants of Antwerp flee to The Netherlands, or to a lesser extent, to Germany. The Spanish pump an enormous amount of money into the Counter-Reformation, enabling Antwerp to remain a cultural centre and home to such artists as Rubens, van Dyck, Jordaens and Teniers.

1715–92
Under Austrian rule Joseph II tries to open the Scheldt to navigation but his attempt fails.

1795
Napoleon succeeds where Joseph II failed.

Antwerp again has open access to the North Sea but is now suffering under the effects of the English blockade.

1792–1815
Napoleon regards Antwerp as 'a gun pointing at the heart of England' and makes it his business to develop it as a modern international port. This is a less fortunate time for its cultural heritage: the French loot or destroy countless works of art.

1830
After the fall of Napoleon, Belgium comes under Dutch rule. When Belgium breaks away from The Netherlands, the port is again faced with a blockade of the Scheldt. Free navigation is restored only in 1863.

1944
During World War II the port of Antwerp escapes devastation, in contrast to Rotterdam. Towards the end of the war the city is, however,

bombarded by VI rockets.

1950 to the present
Since the war the port has been extended systematically towards the north. The construction of the Zandvlietsluis as part of the Ten Year Plan for the port (1956–67) is particularly spectacular. Vessels up to 125,000 tonnes can enter the port through these locks.

The statue of Anthoon (Anthony) van Dyck

Peace & Quiet

In the city

If you want to escape from the hustle and bustle of the city visit the Kruidtuin (▶ 51). There used to be a school of medicine, chemistry and botany next to the St Elisabethziekenhuis (St Elisabeth Hospital) and the plants for the school were grown in this garden. Nowadays it is a botanic garden complete with greenhouses and you can enjoy peace and quiet among remarkable trees, flowers and shrubs.

You can also visit the Stadspark (▶ 111), the largest green space in the centre of the city. The triangular shape of the park reflects the old canal of the Spanish fortifications. The park now includes a lake, a historic suspension bridge, smooth lawns and a playground which is also suitable for visitors with disabilities; for sports fanatics there is a skateboard and roller-skating rink. When the weather is fine you can see the rich with their children and nannies. The park is not far from the diamond quarter (▶ 36).

The inner courts of the Prinsenhof (▶ 59) are beautiful. The Prinsenhof, the former 'Engelsch Huys', belongs to the University of Antwerp and these courtyards can easily stand comparison with the quadrangles of an Oxford or Cambridge college.

The Stadspark in Antwerp

A stroll past the Berg van Barmhartigheid (▶ 32) is very pleasant. In the 16th century the Venusstraat was one of the busiest and most important streets in the city but now it is a peaceful residential neighbourhood with a great atmosphere.

Just outside the city

Across the Ring Road, close to the city centre, lies Antwerp's 'green lung'. It consists of three adjoining parks: Vogelenzang, Middelheim and Den Brandt. All three were once the private pleasure gardens of several noble families. The city bought these areas at the beginning of the 20th century and opened them as parks. Art-lovers will find something to interest them in the Middelheim Openluchtmuseum (open-air museum ▶ 54). In fine weather many local people come here for a stroll, a picnic or simply to relax in green surroundings.

Hortiflora (➤ 110) is a collection of gardens with historical or modern themes. There is, for example, the Dodoenstuin, planted mainly with medicinal herbs and plants. The Rubenstuin was laid out in 1977, the 400th anniversary of the artist's birth. It is in the style of a 16th- and 17th-century aristocrat's garden. Historical sources were consulted to ensure that the plants, the planting scheme and layout are as authentic as possible.

The Kruidtuin, an oasis of quiet in the city

The Kasteel (castle) den Brandt already existed in the 14th century. It was later developed into a pleasure garden for nobles. The city now owns the grounds and the building. A 'Jazz Middelheim' festival is held there every other year. Newly-weds often choose the statue of the dancing nymph in front of the castle as a background for their photographs.

In the 15th century there was a farm on the site of Kasteel Middelheim which three centuries later had developed into a luxurious country house with canals, a lake, stables and a park with statuary – the start of the open-air sculpture museum (➤ 54). The castle now houses a restaurant.

Vogelenzang Park represents only a fraction of the original estate. Most of it disappeared with the construction of the Ring Road round Antwerp. It nevertheless remains a popular family park, particularly on Sundays and sunny holidays. Children never tire of the play area and the lawns beside the little zoo.

Antwerp's Famous

Rubens: Self-Portrait with Hat

Flemish Popular Writer
Hendrik Conscience was the first popular Flemish writer. He was extremely productive because he had to pay for his extravagant lifestyle with his books. Conscience was therefore the first Flemish author to write for a living.

Pieter Paul Rubens (1577–1640)

Painter and diplomat during the baroque period, Rubens was a child of the Reformation. His father, a Calvinist, fled from Antwerp before the Spanish Inquisition. After his death Rubens' mother returned to the city on the Scheldt with her children. The Catholic Rubens was particularly famous for his religious and mythological compositions which were usually commissioned by the Catholic rulers of the city. Rubens the painter was a welcome guest at the European courts where he also carried out diplomatic missions.

Antoon van Dyck (1599–1641)

Protégé of Rubens and assistant in his studio. It was not then unusual for painting to be a matter of 'teamwork', so it is impossible to know how much of the van Dyck's work is concealed in some of Rubens' canvases. Van Dyck's chance came in 1620 when Lady Aletha Talbot took him to England where he was soon established as the court painter of King James I. From then on van Dyck could not go wrong, even when he returned temporarily to Antwerp. 'Sir Anthony' van Dyke was knighted by Charles I in 1632. Van Dyck painted several religious works but remained particularly important as a master portrait painter.

Hendrik Conscience (1812–83)

'He taught his people to read.' Son of a French father and a Flemish mother. He published several poems in French before he finally began to write in Dutch (i.e. Flemish). His most famous novel *De Leeuw van Vlaanderen* (*The Lion of Flanders*) about the Battle of the Spurs in 1302, was actually the first Flemish novel, written in the romantic tradition of that time.

Paul van Ostaijen (1896–1928)

After a none too successful school career, Paul van Ostaijen became city clerk in 1914, thanks to his family's influence. While he was employed by the city he wrote his first collections of poetry. After World War I van Ostaijen had to flee to Berlin because of his pro-German sympathies during the war. Despite being desperately poor he wrote modernist poetry, such as the Dadaist *Bezette Stad* (*Occupied City*, 1921). Van Ostaijen was also the first to translate Kafka from the German. After his return to Belgium he became an art dealer in order to earn his living. He died of tuberculosis at the age of 32.

Top Ten

Above: *a parrot in Antwerp's Zoo*
Right: *the statue of Lange Wapper
on the Steen*

1
Brabo and the Stadhuis on the Grote Markt

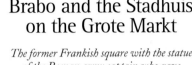

✝ 42A2

✉ Grote Markt 1

☎ 03–2211333

🕐 The Stadhuis can be visited under certain conditions

🚋 2, 3, 4, 7, 8, 10, 11, 15

♿ Good

↔ Carolus Borromeuskerk (➤ 34), Groenplaats (➤ 42), Hendrik Conscienceplein (➤ 46), Onze-Lieve-Vrouwekathedraal (➤ 21)

The former Frankish square with the statue of the Roman army captain who gave Antwerp its name.

During his expedition to Great Britain Julius Caesar left the army captain Silvius Brabo behind to keep an eye on the newly conquered areas. At that time it was said that the settlements along the Scheldt were being terrorized by a cruel giant Druoon Antigoon, who demanded a toll from every skipper who sailed past. If the skipper refused to pay the giant hacked off the man's hand and threw it in the river, hence the name (H)antwerpen or Handwerpen from the Dutch 'to throw'. Silvius Brabo fought the giant, slew him, hacked off his hand and threw it in the river. Historians raise their eyebrows at this story but it remains popular and since 1887 there has been a bronze image of Brabo, made by the master sculptor Jef Lambeaux, on the fountain in the Grote Markt (Market Place). Tourists from all over the world like to have their photographs taken in front of the Brabo Fountain. Several hundred metres further along on the Meir (➤ 109) you can see a recent work of art: *Brabo's Hand*.

The triangular shape of the Grote Markt points to the Frankish origin of the space. Beautiful guild houses surround it. Some of them actually date from the 16th and 17th centuries, others are 19th-century reconstructions built with the aid of contemporary documents, paintings and prints. The painter Antoon van Dyck (➤ 14) was born in No 4, 'den Berendans' in 1599 and in 1493 No 46 was the birthplace of the poet Anna Bijns. The Grote Markt was

The Stadhuis of Antwerp in all its glory, with the Brabo Fountain in the foreground

Grote Markt in Antwerp on a sunny afternoon

not spared the Spanish Fury of 1576. Some of the Gothic guild houses were burned down. They were, however, rebuilt under the succeeding Calvinist regime in a very characteristic South Netherlands style which was to have a great influence abroad.

The Stadhuis (City Hall) must in fact have been a Gothic building, in the tradition of the city halls in Leuven (Louvain) and Brussels. But the building was delayed so often that when another attempt was made in 1560, the wind of humanism was blowing through the city. The Stadhuis had therefore to be built in the new, southern Renaissance style. Cornelis Floris de Vriendt of Antwerp had overall control of the building and later gave his name to the cross between the Gothic and Early Renaissance style: the Floris style. A city hall is expensive: the more than 40 doors on the upper floor were originally small shops that were let in order to pay for the rest of the building – the first boutique arcade in Antwerp.

On the point of the central tower, only vaguely in the Gothic style, you can see an eagle. The eagle is looking towards the imperial city of Aachen: Antwerp was still, as it had been since 963, a frontier province, under the protection of the German Empire. The Madonna in the niche was placed there after the fall of Antwerp; originally there had been a figure of Brabo in the niche. During the Counter-Reformation, however, the Jesuits replaced this statue with one of Our Lady carved by Philips De Vos (1587). The ladies Justice, without a blindfold, and Prudence, embodiment of wisdom, can also be seen.

The interior of the Stadhuis includes several lavishly decorated rooms, much renovated in the 19th century.

2
St Pauluskerk

✚ 30A3

✉ Veemarkt

☎ 03-2323267

🕐 May–Sep 2–5, except
during services

🍴 Excellent cafés
(£–££) and restaurants
(£–££) in the area

🚊 4, 7

♿ Few

✋ Moderate

↔ Internationaal
Zeemanshuis (➤ 48),
Schipperskwartier
(➤ 63)

*A beautiful church with a unique
Calvary on the edge of the
notorious Schipperskwartier.*

St Pauluskerk (St Paul's Church) originally formed part of the
Dominican abbey. It contains beautiful baroque woodcarvings and a fine collection of paintings by 17th-century
masters: Rubens, van Dyck, Jordaens and Francken. The
church also has a famous Calvarieberg (Calvary). It was
commissioned in 1709 by the Van Ketwigh brothers,
themselves Dominican Friars and was carved by the
foremost sculptors of that time: J. de Cock, van Papenhoven,
Quelin and J.P. van Baurscheitsen. The Calvary next to St
Pauluskerk towers over the spot where the bodies from the
nearby gallows-field used to be buried. Another anecdote
about the church relates to the events of the night of 3 April
1968 when the latest and most serious of all the fires it has
suffered took hold. The whole church was ablaze and the
inhabitants and visitors in the nearby seamen's quarter, the
Schipperskwartier (➤ 63) had to save the art treasures. In
his *Guide to Old Antwerp* van Cauwenberg writes: 'The
apocalypse would have been complete had it not been for
the often despised representatives of the seamy side of life,
the night folk, long-haired work-shy riff raff, ladies of ill-
repute, dock workers and seamen of many nationalities who
were the first to force their way into the fire and, risking their
lives, with an instinctive feeling for true value took down the
works of art and dragged them outside.'

*Detail of the Calvary next
to St Pauluskerk*

3
Centraal Station

*The railway cathedral in the heart of
the city. A masterpiece of steel and
glass in neo-Renaissance style.*

✚ 31C3

✉ Diamantstraat

☎ 03–5552555

🕐 Unrestricted

🍴 Excellent cafés
(£–££) in the area

🚊 2, 15

♿ Good

✋ Free

↔ Criée (➤ 35),
Coninckplein (➤ 35),
Diamondland
Showroom (➤ 20),
Gaumont Filmzalen
(➤ 39), Zoo (➤ 26)

Centraal Station (Central Station) is an important feature of the city and is engraved in the collective memory of all its inhabitants. Proud local people even call Centraal Station 'The Railway Cathedral'. The nearby Antwerp Zoo (➤ 26) had to construct a new entrance when the station was built. This beautiful example of Belgian architecture (Louis Delacenserie, 1904) was only just saved from demolition in the 1980s when it was described as a 'heap of rust' and not thought to be worth the cost of restoration. Fortunately opinions changed and about 1993, when Antwerp was the European City of Culture, the station was restored to its former glory.

Order a cup of coffee in the cafeteria. The waiter will repeat your order in a resounding voice for the benefit of the bar staff. At one time this cafeteria was the waiting room for first-class passengers. It gives the impression more of a ballroom in Versailles than a station waiting room. The foyer exudes the atmosphere of an Italian *palazzo*. Many professional photographers use Centraal Station as the setting for their photo sessions: various supermodels have posed on these staircases. You can often see students from the Academy of Fine Arts sketching some of the beautiful details of the building as an exercise.

Centraal Station is a splendid example of art deco architecture with a wealth of detail. This beautiful clock is mounted high in the roof space under a dome of iron and glass

4
Diamond Quarter

✚ 31C3

✉ Diamondland Showroom, Appelmansstraat 33a, 2000 Antwerp

☎ 03–2343612

🕐 Mon–Sat 9:30–5:30, Sun 10–5 (Apr–Oct)

🍴 Excellent cafés (£££) in the area

🚇 2, 15

♿ Few

✋ Free, tour by arrangement

↔ Centraal Station (► 19), Criée (► 35), Coninckplein (► 35), Diamantbuurt (► 36), Gaumont Filmzalen (► 39), Zoo (► 26)

The quarter of the city through which half of the world's cut diamonds have passed, and home to the huge Diamondland Showroom.

Antwerp has been a diamond city since the 16th century when it took over the trade from Bruges, hitherto the European centre of the diamond trade. In the Diamantbuurt (diamond quarter) of Antwerp (► 36) rough, cut and industrial diamonds are traded. The city contains four of the 16 diamond exchanges in the world, and half of all cut diamonds have passed through Antwerp at one time or another. Although most of the stones leave Antwerp to be sold to jewellers all over the world you can, of course, admire and buy them in Antwerp itself. On the fringes of the diamond trade the Antwerp jewellers and diamond cutters have built up an outstanding reputation as vendors of the end product: the cut diamond. The Provincial Diamond Museum (Lange Herentalsstraat 13) traces the history of the trade.

The **Diamondland Showroom** has been set up by the Antwerp Diamond Jewellers Association (ADJA) and is the largest showroom for diamonds in the city. Visitors come from all over the world and tours are arranged in various languages. During the tours you can see diamond cutters, goldsmiths and diamond setters at work. You also learn about the international rules for valuation of the stones according to colour, clarity, cut and carat. The Diamondland Showroom has more than 2,500 gems and uncut diamonds on display. Visitors can also buy diamonds or jewellery. The patronage of the ADJA, under the auspices of the City of Antwerp, acts as a guarantee of quality. If you are going to buy a piece of jewellery elsewhere be sure to ask for the ADJA label.

5

Onze-Lieve-Vrouwekathedraal

The Cathedral of Our Lady, with its 123m-high tower, dominates the Antwerp skyline. Originally there had been plans for a second tower.

In 1352 the plan was to build a separate parish church. Nearly two centuries later, in 1533, the building work was completed. Antwerp was experiencing a period of great prosperity. The cathedral was intended to be much larger, with plans to add a second tower. But after a fire in 1521 the restoration swallowed up so much money that it was never built. In spite of the length of time taken for the building and the various different clients, building was completed in the same Gothic style. Since then the cathedral has suffered various fires and has been ransacked more than once. In 1566 the iconoclasts caused havoc; in 1581 it felt the force of the Calvinist Purification; and in 1794 the French even broke up the floor so that the horses laden with looted works of art should not slip on the smooth stones.

In spite of this history there is still plenty to see, including various works by Rubens: *The Elevation of the Cross*, *The Descent from the Cross*, *The Assumption of the Virgin* and *The Resurrection*. A head of Christ could even be the work of Leonardo da Vinci. The cathedral has beautiful stained-glass windows from the 15th, 16th and 17th centuries.

30B3

Handschoenmarkt

03-2139940

Mon–Fri 10–5, Sat 10–3, Sun and religious holidays 1–4

Excellent cafés (£) and restaurants (£–£££) in the area

2, 3, 4, 7, 8, 10, 11, 15

Good

Reasonable

Carolus Borromeuskerk (➤ 34), Groenplaats (➤ 42), Handschoenmarkt (➤ 43), Hendrik Conscienceplein (➤ 46), Stadhuis (➤ 16)

Onze-Lieve-Vrouwekathedraal with its 123m tower

6
Plantin Moretus Museum

A room in the Plantin Moretus Museum

A museum celebrating a famous printer's family, with authentic 16th-century printing presses.

✝ 42A1

✉ Vrijdagmarkt 22

☎ 03–2330294

🕐 Tue–Sun 10–4:45, Whit Monday and Easter Monday. Closed on 1–2 Jan, 1 May, Ascension Day, 1–2 Nov and 25–26 Dec

🍴 Excellent cafés (£–£££) and restaurants (£–£££) in the area

🚊 2, 3, 4, 7, 8, 10, 11, 15

♿ Few

🖐 Reasonable

↔ Jordaenshuis (► 50), St Annatunnel (► 66), Vlaeykensgang (► 67)

Christopher Plantin, a Frenchman, established his printing house in Kammenstraat in 1555, near where the Dagbladmuseum (► 110) now stands. His first book was an edifying handbook for young ladies. Plantin's business prospered, especially after he became official printer to the Spanish King Philip II. The high point came just before the Spanish Fury (1576, Spanish soldiers went on the rampage), when Plantin had at least 22 presses working. He printed mainly religious works but also dictionaries and academic works. The 'Officina Plantiniana' was then the most famous printing house in Europe. Plantin entertained people such as John Dee, court astrologer of Queen Elizabeth I, Justus Lipsius, Gerard Mercator and Goropius Becanus. Balthasar Moretus was on friendly terms with the painter Rubens, who advised on the design of title pages.

The present Plantin Moretus Museum occupies an 18th-century aristocrat's house that was built by a descendent of the family. It has a lovely 16th-century courtyard but it is particularly worth visiting because of the picture it gives of what artistic, intellectual and economic life was like in the 16th and 17th centuries. You can see authentic old presses and discover how a book was printed in the 16th century. The museum houses a unique collection of books and prints, produced by successive generations of the Moretus family.

7
Rubenshuis

*The house and studio of the master painter
and diplomat with a baroque portico
designed by Rubens himself.*

Rubens bought this house on the Wapper in 1611 and extended it as a dwelling and studio in the style of an Italian *palazzo*. He had previously spent eight years in Italy, as court painter to the Duke of Mantua, and he wanted people to know that. The house was important for promotion: here the painter and diplomat entertained guests and important clients. At the time Rubens was official city painter and court painter to the Archduke Albrecht and his wife Isabella and was developing a splendid career. He still travelled but always returned to this house, where he died in 1640.

The Rubenshuis (Rubens House) is built round a courtyard. The Master himself designed a baroque portico between the inner courtyard and the Flemish-Italianate Renaissance garden. The building changed hands a number of times after his death and the City of Antwerp made repeated attempts to buy it in the 18th and 19th centuries without success until 1937. The house had meanwhile become little more than a ruin and needed massive restoration. You can see how successful this has been because when you enter the building you feel as if you are stepping straight into the 17th century.

In the museum you can admire a number of works by Rubens, including his self portrait, *Adam and Eve in Paradise*, *Hendrik IV's Battle for Paris* and a portrait of the young Antoon van Dyck as a boy.

🕂 30B3

✉ Wapper 9–11

☎ 03–2011555

🕐 Tue–Sun 10–4:45.
Closed on 1–2 Jan,
1 May, Ascension Day,
1–2 Nov and
25–26 Dec

🍴 Excellent cafés (££) and
restaurants (£–£££) in
the area

🚊 2, 3, 15

♿ Good

✋ Moderate

↔ Koninklijk Paleis (► 51),
Osterriethhuis (► 58),
St Jacobskerk (► 24),
Vogelenmarkt (► 68)

*The entrance to
the Rubenshuis on
the Wapper*

8
St Jacobskerk

The last resting place of the painter Rubens. The tower of St Jacobskerk was to have been taller than that of the Onze-Lieve-Vrouwekathedraal.

St Jacobskerk, which has the richest church interior in the city

✚ 30B3

✉ Lange Nieuwstraat 73

☎ 03-2321032

🌐 15 Apr–31 Oct: Mon–Sat 12–5, Sun and holidays 1–5; Nov–Mar: Mon–Fri 9–12. Closed to visitors during services

🍴 Excellent cafés (£–£££) and restaurants (£–£££) in the area

🚊 2, 3, 15

♿ Good

✋ Moderate

↔ Koninklijk Paleis (►51),Osterriethhuis (►58), Rubenshuis (►23), Vogelenmarkt (►68)

The biggest attraction in this church is the grave of Pieter Paul Rubens, but there is so much else to see. The interior is indisputably the richest interior of all among the churches of the city, simply because unlike other churches it was not ransacked by the French occupying forces. St Jacobskerk (St Jacob's Church) was conceived as a prestige project when it was built between 1491 and 1656. The area of the Lange Nieuwstraat was then the home of the upper classes, merchants and nobles, and their specific aim was to build a church with a tower 'taller than the cathedral'. The honourable gentlemen did not succeed in their plan. For financial reasons the tower reached only 55m.

Within the church, however, there is no lack of splendour; here the nouveau riche and the old aristocracy could compete with each other, instead of joining forces to pay for a tower. More than a hundred types of marble were worked into the interior of St Jacobskerk and the work was carried out by the very best craftsmen.

All the important artists in Antwerp at that time contributed a work of art here. There are 23 chapels in the church. Rubens grave is behind the high altar in the Lady Chapel. He painted the canvas *Madonna and Child with Saints* for his own memorial. According to experts, it is a disguised family portrait, with Rubens as St George.

9
The Steen

The oldest building still standing in Antwerp,
now the Nationale Scheepvaartmuseum
(National Maritime Museum).

Het Steen (the Steen, literally 'the stone') as we now know it dates from 1200 and was intended as a stone reinforcement for the original earth and timber defences. This wall was built after the Norman raid on the settlement by the Scheldt in 836. The Steen is the oldest building still standing in Antwerp. Charles V had the fortress renovated in 1540. Evidence of this can still be seen in the coat of arms of the emperor and his motto *Plus Oultre* above the entrance to the museum. Above the gateway you can also see a small statue of Semini, the Scandinavian god of youth and fertility. For a long time the Steen also served as a prison and the crucifix opposite the entrance dates from this period. Those condemned to death could murmur their last prayers here on the way to the gallows. The Steen was the only building spared when the quays were laid out in the 19th century. The remainder of the old city, with 600 houses, finally disappeared. The Steenplein is now a peaceful place by the water where the cruise boats of the shipping company Flandria are moored (▶110).

Nowadays the Steen houses the National Maritime Museum (▶111). The collection includes old and modern model ships, charts, prints, maritime equipment and so on. Next to the Steen there is a collection of boats and cranes. Regular exhibitions are held in one boat, the *Lauranda*. This is part of the open-air section of the Maritime Museum, together with the harbour equipment.

✚ 42A2

✉ Steenplein 1

☎ 03–2320850

🕐 Tue–Sun 10–4:45, Whit Monday and Easter Monday. Closed on 1–2 Jan, 1 May, Ascension Day, 1–2 Nov, 25–26 Dec

🍴 Excellent cafés (£–£££) and restaurants (£–£££) in the area

🚊 2, 3, 4, 7, 15

♿ Good

↔ Hanzahuis (▶44), Hangars (▶44), Stadhuis (▶16), Groenplaats (▶42)

The Steen, the oldest building in Antwerp

10
The Zoo

*An elephant in
Antwerp Zoo*

*One of the oldest and most famous zoos in
the world in the heart of the city, just
next to the Centraal Station.*

When Antwerp Zoo was built in 1843 it was just outside the city boundary. The original land occupied only one hectare but before the Zoo was even finished its extension began. The first director of the Zoo was the then famous zoologist and botanist Jacques Kets. Kets accepted the position only on the condition that he could have a museum for his own natural history collection. The Zoo has continued to grow to ten times its original area until the city overtook it. In 1904, Centraal Station (► 19) was built just beside the Zoo, and a new entrance had to be made.

As well as many animals the Zoo is well landscaped and can boast several splendid examples of 19th-century architecture. It is certainly worth visiting the Egyptian temple (1856) for elephants and giraffes and the antelope building (1861) which now houses okapis. After World War II the Zoo was completely reorganised to satisfy new scientific, educational, cultural and aesthetic requirements: for example, the animal houses were made lighter and more spacious. Additions included a building for the anthropoid apes, a complex for birds of prey, a special house where nocturnal animals can be observed in darkness, and a complex for dolphins (1968). In 1973 a completely new reptile house was built. Nowadays the Zoo takes part in international breeding programmes for endangered animal species. It is famous for its scientific research and the Royal Society for Animals has to guarantee that the animals can live under the best possible conditions.

The Zoo also has a planetarium, a winter garden, an aquaforum and a chilled area for penguins. It is a great attraction, especially for children.

✚ 31C3

✉ Koningin Astridplein 26

☎ 03–2024540

🕓 Daily from 9, closing time varies according to season

🍴 Excellent cafés (£–££) in the area

🚇 2, 15

♿ Excellent

✋ Moderate

↔ Centraal Station (► 19), Criée (► 35), Coninckplein (► 35), Diamondland Showroom (► 20), Gaumont Filmzalen (► 39)

What To See

Above: touring in style through the heart of Antwerp

Left: a stone camel rider above the entrance to the Zoo

Antwerp

Antwerp is full of beautiful things to see, but above all it is a living city. The Cathedral of Our Lady stands proudly and companionably between the Oudaan and the Boerentoren, two modern peaks of the Antwerp skyline. The architectural development of the city has never come to a halt, probably because of its turbulent economic and political past. At various times in the past the city was so little aware of its cultural heritage that space was always being made for renewal. So splendid buildings, lovely places disappeared forever. But as you wander round the city today you never have the feeling that you are walking about in a time capsule. The city has retained its vitality. It is only a step or two from the historic centre to the Meir, the shopping street, and after visiting the outstanding museums in the city you can enjoy the dazzling nightlife.

> *'This building is worth a kingdom, you must keep it carefully in a case and only show it to the people once a year.'*
>
> EMPEROR CHARLES V
> on Onze-Lieve-Vrouwekathedraal
> in Antwerp

Antwerp

Antwerp is several cities all at the same time. There is Antwerp the seaport, the economic artery not only for Greater Antwerp but also for a hinterland that stretches deep into Flanders. There is Antwerp the city of culture, past and present. For others Antwerp is the world's principal diamond city: for years an international trade has flourished here, making a considerable contribution to the Belgian Gross National Product. In addition, Antwerp has become a city of fashion since the emergence of the 'Antwerp Six' group of designers (➤ 106). And there is much, much more.

Antwerp Tourist Office is housed behind this typical Flemish facade

Whichever Antwerp you choose, there is always much to discover. The city is bursting with historic buildings, so much so that the locals themselves are not aware of them all. A visitor once commented: 'You only have to open a door and there is something lovely behind it'. That is often the case. Antwerp houses countless treasures from the past and is still a vibrant city of culture. A number of the most important contemporary Flemish artists live and work in Antwerp. Belgian fashions sometimes seem to coincide with Antwerp fashions. The city remains an economic giant: the port stretches from the district of Antwerp North almost to the Dutch border; the continuous loading and unloading of containers provides constant activity and contributes to Antwerp's well-being. This ensures that Antwerp is a fine, lively place: shopping on the Meir among throngs of people is a delight, and in the evening you can see why Antwerp attracts people from a wide area. The people of Antwerp have always been able to value the good life and they are happy to let visitors share in their enjoyment.

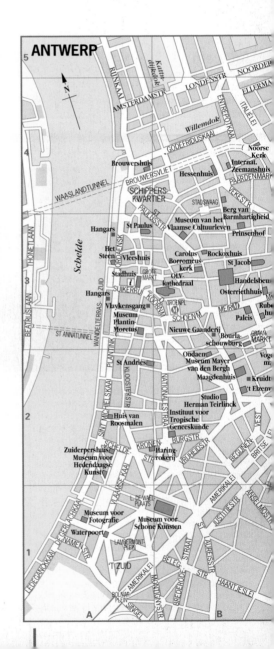

VIADUCT-DAM

VISESTR

HALENSTR

STR

ORANJE-

STUIVENBERG-
PLEIN

OUDE STEENW

VAN KERCKHOVENSTR

ONDERWIJSSTRAAT

POTHOEKSTR

DIEPESTR

HANDELSSTR

BEELDEKENSSTR

LANGE

KERK-

STRAAT

DE CONINC-
PL

VAN W. STR

HELMSTRAAT

Criée

GEMEENTE-   STR

CARNOTSTR

TURNHOUTSEBAAN

KON. ASTRIDPL

BORGERHOUT

Opera

Gaumont
Filmzalen

■ Zoo

KEYSERLEI

Centraal
Station

Diamondland
Showroom

DIAMANTSTR

PLOEGSTR

PROVINCIESTRAAT

QUINTEN MATSIJSLEI

Stadspark

PLANTIN EN MORETUSLEI

VAN EYCKLEI

LOOS-
PLAATS BRIALMONTLEI

MERCATORSTR

ARENDSSTR

Cogels-Osylei

CHARLOTTALEI

CUPERUSSTR

LANGE   LEEMSTRAAT

MECHELSE STEENWEG

BELGIELEI

LAMORINIERSTRAAT

BERCHEM

BOOMGAARDSTRAAT

Koning
Albert-
park

0   250   500 m

C   D

What to See in Antwerp

🏳 30B3
✉ Minderbroedersstraat 22
☎ 03–2325580
🕐 Tue–Fri 10–4:45. Closed
on feast days
🍴 Excellent cafés (£–££)
and restaurants (£–£££)
in the area
🚋 4, 7 🚌 9, 6/34
♿ Good 🚼 Moderate
↔ Berg van Barmhartig-
heid (➤ 32),
Hessenhuis (➤ 47),
Prinsenhor (➤ 59),
Stadswaag (➤ 66)

ARCHIEF EN MUSEUM VAN HET VLAAMSE CULTUURLEVEN ✪

The Archives and Museum of Flemish Culture houses a large collection of archives behind an 18th-century facade in the former auction rooms of the Antwerp baliffs. You can find a wonderful over-view of 200 years of Flemish culture, in the form of old photographs, sculptures and paintings, historical documents, and even reconstructions of the studies of notable Flemish writers. The museum inherited the art collection of Hendrik Conscience (➤ 14). The Archives and Museum of Flemish Culture is also one of the most important centres for documentation in connection with the Flemish Movement.

Head of the Flemish poet Karel van de Woestijne in the Archives and Museum of Flemish Culture

BERG VAN BARMHARTIGHEID (and surroundings) ✪

In the 16th century, Venusstraat was one of the busiest and most important streets, especially after the construction of the Stadswaag (➤ 66). This importance is illustrated even today by many gables and inner courtyards. which are an indirect result of the fall of Antwerp in 1585. Well-to-do Catholic families who had not fled in the face of the Spaniards bought the land and houses in the area for a song and erected large houses in their place. The Berg van Barmhartigheid was a pawnbrokers (1620). It was set up as an alternative to the usury practices which flourished despite being banned by the church in the 16th and 17th centuries. People were able to pawn their belongings at a relatively low rate of interest. The pawnbroker's shop remained open until World War II. Venusstraat is now a peaceful residential area and one of the most pleasant parts of Antwerp.

🏳 30B4
✉ Venusstraat 13
☎ None
🕐 Private house, please
respect the privacy of
the residents
🍴 Excellent cafés (£–££)
and restaurants (£–£££)
in the area
🚋 4, 7 🚌 9, 6/34
♿ Few
↔ Archief en Museum
van het Vlaamse
Cultuurleven (➤ 32),
Prinsenhof (➤ 59),
Stadswaag (➤ 66),
Hessenhuis (➤ 47)

BOERENTOREN ✪✪

In the 1930s this must have been the first and tallest skyscraper in Europe – the people of Antwerp would not settle for anything less. There was one restriction, the city fathers wanted a modern and monumental building but not so monumental that it would dominate or obscure the nearby cathedral (► 21). The architect looked to New York and Chicago for his inspiration and used steel frame construction because then the building could be higher without the need for many points of support on the ground. At that time the people of Antwerp were very proud of their skyscraper.

The name of the building comes from the first occupant: the Boerenbank.

➕ 42B1
✉ Hoek Schoenmarkt–Eiermarkt
🕐 Can only be viewed from outside
🍴 Excellent cafés (£–££) and restaurants (£–£££)
🚊 4, 8
♿ 🚇
↔ Handelsbeurs (► 43), Onze-Lieve-Vrouwekathedraal (► 21)

Below: *the restored Bourlaschouwburg in all its splendour*

BOURLASCHOUWBURG ✪✪✪

The architect Pierre Bruno Bourla built this theatre just after 1830 in the heart of the Latin Quarter, so called because it was the centre of entertainment for the French-speaking bourgeoisie. The Bourlaschouwburg later fell into disrepair and was only reopened in 1993 after a thorough restoration. It is now the home of the city theatre company, the Toneelhuis (► 112). In the foyer on the first floor you can order coffee and cakes and daydream in the elegant pre-war surroundings.

➕ 30B3
✉ Komedieplaats 18
☎ 03–2310750
🍴 Excellent cafés (£–££) and restaurants (£–£££)
🚊 7, 8 ♿ Few
💷 Expensive
↔ Graanmarkt (► 40), Maagdenhuis (► 53)

✚ 30A4
✉ Adriaan Brouwersstraat 20
☎ 03–2326511
⏱ Only open to groups, by appointment
🍴 Excellent cafés (£–££) and restaurants (£–££) in the area
🚋 4, 7 ♿ Few
🎫 Moderate
↔ Godefriduskaai (➤ 40)

BROUWERSHUIS

The Brouwershuis (Brewer's House) was actually the Waterhuis (Water House) for the various breweries in the vicinity. For three centuries from the 16th century it was the distribution centre for water. The equipment is still largely intact: a horse-powered treadmill hauled up the water to the channels on the top floor and from there it was fed to the surrounding breweries via an ingenious system of pipes. The designer was the 16th-century engineer and land speculator Gilbert van Schoonbeke. He hardly reached the age of 37 but he built more than 23 streets, two squares and in this area a whole new neighbourhood. The boardroom of the brewery on the first floor is decorated with gold leather from Mechelen (Malines). The room used to contain a famous painting by Hendrik de Braeckeleer, which depicts an old man sitting dreaming by a window. At present the painting hangs in the Koninklijke Museum van Schone Kunsten (➤ 51).

ST PAULUSKERK (➤ 18, TOP TEN)

Below: *interior of the Carolus Borromeuskerk, showing the high altar*

✚ 42B2
✉ Hendrik Conscienceplein, 2000 Antwerp
☎ 03–2313751
⏱ Variable opening times, see board at entrance
🍴 Excellent cafés (£–££) and restaurants (£–£££)
🚋 2, 3, 4, 7, 8, 10, 11, 15
♿ Few
↔ Hendrik Conscienceplein (➤ 46), Onze-Lieve-Vrouwekathedraal (➤ 21), Stadhuis (➤ 16)

CAROLUS BORROMEUSKERK

A triumph of the Reformation, the Jesuits built this magnificent baroque church to bring the faithful back into the fold after the fall of Antwerp (1621). Rubens was involved in the decoration of the facade. The church was originally clad in coloured marble but after the fire of 1718 it was re-clad more soberly. No less than 39 works by Rubens went up in flames that year. The extension of the high altar is by Peter van Baurscheit the elder, as is the pulpit and the case of the Forceville organ. The painting above the altar can be changed using an original mechanism which is still in working order. At 11:30 every Sunday morning there is an Artists' Mass with a musical setting.

CENTRAAL STATION (➤ 19, TOP TEN)

DID YOU KNOW?

Carolus Borromeuskerk only got its present name after the possessions of the Jesuits were declared forfeit. In 1773 the building took on a new use under the patronage of the 16th Archbishop of Milan, Carlo Borromeo.

CRIÉE ⭐

In the heart of Antwerp's Chinatown, Van Wesebekestraat (► 67), market traders and shopkeepers sell top quality fresh fish, meat, poultry and vegetables. The covered market has a southern atmosphere. The iron roof structure is the 19th-century original. The name comes from the French *crier* meaning 'to call'. Until a fire in 1983, poultry and game were sold by auction.

Tourists like to come to look round because of the market's atmosphere and to see Chinatown, but most of the visitors to Criée are local people who come here simply to do their shopping.

➕ 31C3
✉ Van Schoonhovenstraat 21
🕐 Mon–Sat 10–6, Sun closed
🍴 Excellent cafés (£–££)
🚊 2, 15 ♿ Few
✋ Free
↔ Centraal Station (► 19), De Coninckplein (► 35), Diamondland Showroom (► 20), Gaumont Film-zalen (► 39), Zoo (► 26)

DE CONINCKPLEIN ⭐

A triangular plain in the middle of the station neighbourhood. Young people play basketball here during the day. For years De Coninckplein was a place where people could go in the small hours for a snack or entertainment. Nowadays it is a more lurid centre of entertainment with videogame arcades and a number of lively African bars. It is also the centre of the African community in Antwerp. De Coninckplein comes out into Van Wesenbekestraat (► 67), Antwerp's Chinatown. Chinese holidays, such as the Chinese New Year, are always celebrated here.

➕ 31C4
🍴 Excellent cafés (£–££) in the area
🚊 2, 15
♿ Few
✋ Free
↔ Centraal Station (► 19), Criée (► 35), Gaumont Filmzalen (► 39), Zoo (► 26)

Above: *a facade in Criée*

35

➕ Not on the map

✉ Corner of Generaal Van Merlenstraat and Waterloostraat

🍴 Excellent cafés (£–££) and restaurants (£–££) in the area

🚋 11, 8

↔ Draakplaats (➤ 38), Gouvernementsgebouw (➤ 40)

The Four Seasons, detail from the 'Autumn' house

DE VIER SEIZOENEN

One of the most attractive corners of Antwerp. The four corner houses: Spring, Summer, Autumn and Winter which were designed by the same architect (Bascourt 1899) together form a whole. Sadly some of the original decoration has disappeared. Each 'season' has its own colour: shades of green for Spring and Summer, shades of brown for Autumn and Winter. Although the houses appear identical, they are not. You can look for the differences yourself. One tip: the mosaics and the stained-glass windows have faces and signs of the zodiac and flowers connected with the theme of the house. The low garden walls allow the trees in the garden to spill over into the street.

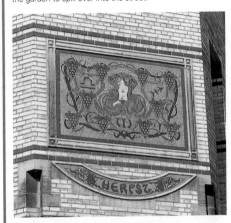

➕ 31C3

✉ Appelmansstraat, Lange Herentalsestraat, Schupstraat, Hoveniersstraat, Rijfstraat, Vestingstraat, Pelikaanstraat.

🕐 Free, tour by appointment

🍴 Excellent cafés (£–££)

🚋 2, 15 ♿ Reasonable

💷 Free

↔ Centraal Station (➤ 19), Criée (➤ 35), De Coninckplein (➤ 35), Diamondland Showroom (➤ 20), Gaumont Filmzalen (➤ 39), Zoo (➤ 26)

DIAMANTBUURT

Half of all rough, cut or industrial diamonds pass through Antwerp and 'Cut in Antwerp' is the most prestigious international label for cut diamonds. Yet not a trace of a diamond has been found in excavations in Antwerp. It was the Arabs and Persians who brought diamonds to the city. In the 13th century, diamonds were brought across the Rhine via Venice to Bruges, at that time the centre of the diamond trade and diamond working. After the Zwin silted up Bruges no longer had a reliable harbour and the trade moved to Antwerp, there to stay. The Diamantbuurt (Diamond Quarter) is well worth a short stroll. Allow yourself to be caught up in the stream of Jewish, Indian and Asiatic dealers. The Diamondland Showroom (➤ 20) in the heart of the quarter is worth visiting as is the Provincial Diamond Museum (➤ 20).

A Walk Through the Centre of Antwerp

Start at the Grote Markt.

You can have a drink looking out over the Brabo Fountain (► 16) and the Stadhuis (► 16).

Leave the Stadhuis behind and walk in the direction of the Handschoenmarkt.

The Onze-Lieve-Vrouwekathedraal (► 21) here is certainly worth a visit.

Go from Handschoenmarkt into Oude Korenmarkt. Above the entrance to No 16 hangs a small shield with Vlaeykensgang on it, enter here. Go through Vlaeykensgang to Pelgrimstraat and follow this to Reyndersstraat to reach the Groenplaats.

Groenplaats (► 42) is very popular with local people as well as tourists. It contains the statue of Rubens (► 62).

Cross Groenplaats diagonally and leave it via St Pietersstraat. Turn left into Melkmarkt, walk on to Korte Koepoortstraat and then turn right into Wijngaardstraat.

Wijngaardstraat runs alongside Hendrik Conscienceplein (► 46), one of Antwerp's most attractive small squares. This is a good place to eat or drink in one of the cafés or restaurants. The Carolus Borromeuskerk (► 34) is well worth a visit.

At the end of Wijngaardstreet turn left into Wolstraat and keep straight on; the Wolstraat becomes Oude Beurs. At the end of Oude Beurs turn right into Vleeshouwersstraat.

The route goes past the Vleeshuis (► 68).

Follow Vleeshouwersstraat to Zakstraat and turn left into it. Cross the Jordaenskaai to the Steenplein.

Since the Scheldt was straightened out in the 19th century and the medieval city centre disappeared except for the Steen, the Jordaenskaai has formed the boundary between the city and the river

Distance
2km

Time
2–4 hours

Start/end point
Grote Markt–Steenplein
✚ 30A–B3
🚊 2, 3, 15, 4, 8

Lunch
't Brantijser (££)
✉ Hendrik Conscienceplein 7
☎ 03–2331833

⊞ Not on the map
¶¶ Excellent cafés and
restaurants in the area
🚃 11, 8
↔ De Vier Seizoenen
(► 36), Gouvernements-
gebouw (► 40)

DRAAKPLAATS

The water towers, beside the railway line, used to supply water for steam locomotives. They are now listed as examples of industrial archaeology and are city landmarks. Everything in this square points to the heyday of public transport. The offices and depots of the municipal tram company date back to the era of the horse-drawn tram, when it was very important to have good connections with the centre. At one time there were two competing transport companies and each with their terminus in this square. Close by are the Cogels-Osylei and Transvaalstraat with their houses with huge gables. It was then considered smart to live near the railway.

'T ELZENVELD

This was a hospital by the 13th century. Nowadays it is a conference centre with an exhibition hall. The cloister and the former wards contain old paintings and antique furniture. Not long ago a unique wall painting was found in the former chapel. The old tiled kitchens are certainly worth a visit.

⊞ 30B2
✉ Lange Gasthuisstraat 45
☎ 03–2235620
🕐 Groups only, by
appointment
¶¶ Excellent cafés and
restaurants in the area
🚃 7, 8 **♿** Good
💲 Cheap
↔ Bourlaschouwburg
(► 33), Maagdenhuis
(► 53)

The old water towers on Draakplaats, now listed as examples of industrial archaeology

ETNOGRAFISCH MUSEUM ✪✪

Antwerp has always had a privileged connection with the world beyond Europe because of its port and you can explore the four continents for yourself in this Museum of Ethnography. There are everyday objects, works of art and religious artefacts that tell the story of these non-European cultures. The whole collection, which began in 1864, contains 25,000 items and is still growing. Among the most interesting objects are masks and woodcarvings from Africa, Indonesian weapons, Indian sculptures, bronzes and scroll paintings from the Himalayas. A number of the objects are unique in the world.

GAUMONT FILMZALEN ✪

The first cinema opened its doors in 1906 in the Stationsbuurt (station quarter) and since then 'doing a cinema' has been for the people in Antwerp synonymous with seeing a film and then going out on the town. Many cinemas in the centre closed in the 1980s. In 1997, however, Gaumont opened the largest urban cinema complex in Europe with 17 screens. Since then Antwerp has again been able to call itself a 'cinema city'. From the top storey of the Gaumont complex there is a wonderful panorama of the station quarter.

➕ 42A2
✉ Suikerrui 19
☎ 03–2208600
🕐 Tue–Sun 10–4:45, Easter Monday and Whit Monday. Closed on 1–2 Jan, 1 May, 15 Aug, 1–2 Nov, 25–26 Dec
🍴 Excellent cafés and restaurants in the area
♿ Few
✋ Cheap
↔ Grote Markt (➤ 16), the Steen (➤ 25)

African art in the Antwerp Museum of Ethnography

➕ 31C3
✉ Van Ertbornstraat 17
☎ 03–2067000
🕐 Open until last film showing
🍴 Excellent cafés (£–£££) and restaurants (£–£££) in the area
🚌 2, 15
♿ Few
✋ Moderate
↔ Centraal Station (➤ 19), Coninckplein (➤ 35), Zoo (➤ 26)

The Gaumont Filmzalen, the largest urban cinema complex in Europe

GODEFRIDUSKAAI ✪

'Het Eilandje' (the Little Island), the old warehouse quarter between city and port is undergoing a revival. The lovely 19th-century warehouses on the Willemsdok each have a name: Marnix (1865), Godfried (1905), St Felix (1863), Michiels-Loos (1863) and Rubens Noord (1858). Very recently a number of warehouses were converted into offices or lofts for young professionals.

GOUVERNEMENTSGEBOUW ✪

Gouvernementsgebouw (Government House, 1906), in fact seven houses, is a copy of Government House in the Transvaal, South Africa. At the beginning of the 20th century people still regarded the Boer War as a heroic struggle against the British occupying forces and the Boers could count on a great deal of sympathy in Antwerp. The garden behind the building backs on to the railway line to The Netherlands. Living close to the railway was very fashionable in those days. While the facade is built of stone, the back of the building is faced with plasterwork; this was a money-saving measure.

*Gouvernementsgebouw
is an exact copy of
Government House in
the Transvaal, South Africa*

GRAANMARKT ✪

One of the prettiest little squares in the city, near the Kruidtuin (➤ 51) and the Bourlaschouwburg (➤ 33). Graanmarkt was already in existence in 1552 when it was known as Brabantse Corenmarkt; the step gables of houses Nos 1, 3 and 5 are reminders of that period. In 1980 Graanmark was refurbished and laid out again. In the centre there is a statue of Victor Driessens, a pioneer in the life of Dutch-language theatre.

A Walk to Antwerp South and Back

View of a sun-drenched Marnixplaats in the heart of Antwerp South

Begin at the Modepaleis (➤ 107), Nationalestraat 16, on the corner of Kammenstraat. Modepaleis is the home of the fashion designer Dries van Noten.

Cross over Nationalestraat to the extension of Kammenstraat and follow this through. Kammenstraat becomes Begijnenstraat. At the end of Begijnenstraat turn right into Kronenburgstraat.

On the way there are all kinds of stylish clothing shops; leaving the police tower Oudaan (➤ 58) to the left go past Antwerp prison on the right. The Instituut voor Tropishce Geneeskunde (Institute of Tropical Medicine ➤ 48) is by the traffic lights 100m down Kronenburgstraat.

Half way down Kronenburgstraat turn left into Lambermontstraat. Cross over Marnixplaats to K. Rogierstraat and emerge on to Leopold De Waelplaats

You can visit the Koninklijk Museum voor Schone Kunsten (Royal Museum of Fine Arts ➤ 51), relax in one of the cafés in the area or have something to eat.

Leave Leopold De Waelplaats via Van Egmonstraat and come out in Kloosterstraat which you can stroll down.

Kloosterstraat (➤ 50) is a mecca for antiques and souvenirs in Antwerp.

Distance
4 km

Time
4–6 hours

Start point
Nationalestraat 16
➕ 30B2
🚊 4, 8

End point
Kloosterstraat
➕ 30B2
🚊 4, 8

Lunch
Fairfood (££)
✉ Graaf Van Egmontstraat 60
☎ 03–2389296

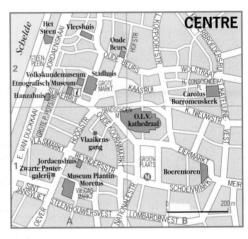

✚ 42B2
✉ Groenplaats
🕐 Unrestricted
🍴 Excellent cafés and restaurants (£–£££)
🚃 2, 15 ♿ Few
🔁 Grote Markt with the Brabo Fountain (► 16), Stadhuis (► 16)

GROENPLAATS

✪✪✪

Groenplaats was a churchyard until 1784. Old residents of Antwerp still refer to it as 't Groen Kerkhof' (the green churchyard). In 1803 the square was inaugurated as 'Place Bonaparte', a name it lost when Napoleon tasted defeat. People have called it Groenplaats, a translation of 'Place Verte' since the city fathers decided to plant trees in the space. Meanwhile the trees have disappeared from the square, something that these same old residents refer to as 'a disgrace'.

Nowadays Groenplaats, with its many cafés in the shadow of Onze-Lieve-Vrouwekathedraal (► 21) is a favourite spot for tourists. There is a daily flower market and street musicians add to the atmosphere. In the centre is a statue of Rubens (► 62), a meeting place for 'alternative' youth and skaters.

GROTE MARKT WITH THE BRABO FOUNTAIN
(► 16, TOP TEN)

HANDELSBEURS ✪
The Antwerp exchange was founded in 1531 and was later the model for the stock exchanges in Amsterdam and London. Antwerp experienced its financial Golden Age when the city took over control from Bruges, until then the financial centre of the north. At the exchange in Antwerp the financial agents of royal houses such as the Valois, the Tudors and the Habsburgs speculated together with English, Italian, Spanish, Portuguese, French and Dutch merchants and of course those from Antwerp itself. They traded in spices and exotica from the overseas colonies, textiles from Italy and England and wine and metalwork from Germany. The end of the Golden Age for Antwerp came with the death of Emperor Charles V (1555). Religious wars, always bad for trade, broke out under his successor Philip II. The exchange building later became an academy of arts, then the first public library in Antwerp. It is now sporadically a location for banquets and other events.

- ✚ 30B3
- ✉ Twaalfmaandenstraat
- 🕐 Exterior only can be viewed
- 🍽 Excellent cafés and restaurants (£–£££) in the area
- 🚊 4, 8
- ↔ Boerentoren (► 33), Groenplaats (► 42)

HANDSCHOENMARKT ✪✪
Handschoenmarkt was formerly a churchyard which was referred to as 'Small or Stone Churchyard'. From the 16th century there were stalls selling gloves there – hence its name meaning 'glove market'. Now it contains a couple of outstanding restaurants, a number of lively facades – not always well restored – and the *Put van Quinten Metsijs*. This interwoven wrought-iron canopy from 1490 used to cover the well in front of the old City Hall. According to legend, Quinten Metsys, for love of a painter's daughter, changed his blacksmith's craft to painting. Notice the image of Brabo in the metalwork. Throw a coin in the well and make a wish.

On Monday evenings during the summer months you can listen to a carillon concert from the bells of the Onze-Lieve-Vrouwekathedraal. These carillon concerts give the residents of Antwerp another excuse to sit outdoors at a pavement café in Handschoenmarkt.

- ✚ 42A1
- ✉ Handschoenmarkt
- 🕐 Unrestricted
- 🍽 Excellent cafés and restaurants (£–£££) in the area
- 🚊 2, 15 ♿ Good
- ↔ Onze-Lieve-Vrouwe-kathedraal (► 21), Grote Markt with the Brabo Fountain (► 16), Stadhuis (► 16)

Left: *the statue of Rubens on Groenplaats*

43

HANGARS ⊕⊕

30A3–4

✉ Wandelterras Zuid and Wandelterras Noord

🕐 Unrestricted

🍴 Excellent cafés and restaurants (£–£££)

🚊 2, 3, 4, 7 15 ♿ None

↔ Hanzahuis (► 44), Stadhuis (► 16), the Steen (► 25), Groenplaats (► 42)

In 1885 these 3.5km-long wharves were built. They were fenced off but two terraces were constructed by the port authorities to allow people to view the activities. The residents of Antwerp gazed with fascination at the busy harbour below: exotic goods that were being unloaded and the strange people arriving. Today the wharves are almost deserted. The 'hangars' (sheds) have become parking spaces or exhibition areas for displaying old ships. Strolling along the terraces you can still sense some of the atmosphere of the 'Old Scheldt'.

HANZAHUIS ⊕

42A2

✉ Hoek Suikerrui–Ernest Van Dijckkaai

🕐 Can only be viewed externally

🍴 Excellent cafés and restaurants in the area

↔ Hangars (► 44), Stadhuis (► 16), the Steen (► 25), Groenplaats (► 42)

Above: *the atmospheric hangars today serve as parking places*

Hansa House was one of the first office buildings in the city. Built in neo-baroque style, the mythical figures represent the god of trade, Mercury; they were modelled by the sculptor Lambeaux, also famous for the Brabo Fountain (► 16).

> ### DID YOU KNOW?
>
> Until the Napoleonic era houses had no number, just a name. This was not only painted on the house front as house numbers are today, but also depicted on a facing brick on the gable. It is fun to look out for them.

A Walk Along the Scheldt Wharves

Leave the Steenplein beside the Steen (► 25).

Walk up to the south terrace and follow it all the way.

There are telescopes here and for a small coin you can have a view across the Scheldt to the left bank.

At the end of the south terrace go down, follow the Plantinkaai to the right but turn right again immediately in order to follow the Scheldt below. This is Scheldt Wharf 18a and you follow the Scheldt to Scheldt Wharf 15a.

Walk on the blue pavement, as close to the water as possible. Be careful. Look down: the Scheldt was and is the artery of Antwerp. You walk along the back of Magic World, Antwerp in miniature (► 110).

At Scheldt Wharf 15a, cross past IJzeren Poort Wharf to the Waalse Wharf and from there to the Vlaamse quay on the other side of the square.

The area between the Vlaamse and Waalse Wharves is a former dock that has been filled in. The Provinciaal Museum voor Fotografie (Provincial Museum of Photography ► 54) is situated here together with many cafés and small restaurants.

Follow the Vlaamse Wharf up to the left and straight on to Kloosterstraat, and continue to Hoogstraat.

Distance
4km

Time
4–6 hours

Start/End point
The Steen–Hoogstraat
✚ 30A3
🚊 2, 3, 4

Lunch
Entrepot du Congo (££)
✉ Vlaamsekaai 42
☎ 03–2389232

You can get a beautiful view of the left bank from the quays; residents of Antwerp like to come here for a breath of fresh air

🕆 30A–B2
✉ Kronenburgstraat 34
☎ 03-2481577
🕓 By appointment
🍴 Cafés and restaurants
🚃 7, 8
♿ Few

🕆 42B2
✉ Hendrik Conscienceplein
🍴 Good cafés and restaurants
🚃 2, 3, 4, 7, 8, 10, 11, 15
♿ Good
↔ Carolus Borromeuskerk (➤ 34), Onze-Lieve-Vrouwe-kathedraal (➤ 21), Stadhuis (➤ 16)

Above: *the herring smokehouse with its tall chimneys is now a residential project*

Hendrik Conscienceplein with the Carolus Borromeuskerk

HARINGROKERIJ ✪

This was originally an industrial complex where herring, eels and halibut were salted and smoked in the tall chimneys. In 1986 six families jointly bought the listed building and converted it into a unique housing complex, with communal facilities and a garden.

HENDRIK CONSCIENCEPLEIN ✪✪✪

One of the most attractive small squares in Antwerp. Most of the buildings, including the beautiful Carolus Borromeuskerk (➤ 34) are the result of the 17th-century Jesuits' passion for building. The Jesuits had their own agenda. They spared neither money nor effort to recall the residents of Antwerp to the faith – after more than a century of raging religious argument – in this case to the Catholic Church. There is a statue of Hendrik Conscience (➤ 14) in the centre of the cobbled square. In the 1960s Hendrik Conscience-plein was a centre of alternative entertainment and the local residents and artists organised demonstrations against cars. The square was the first pedestrian precinct in the city.

HESSENHUIS ✪✪✪

The city built the Hessenhuis (Hessen House) at No 53 Falconrui, a street where there are also two 16th- and 17th-century hospices. At the time Antwerp was flourishing (1563–65) and the German Hansa traders were asking for somewhere to store their goods and unload their wagons. The name comes from the workers who were involved in loading and unloading the Hessen wagons. Stables and storage occupied the ground floor, the drivers lived on the first floor, and their wagons were parked on the area outside.

Hessen House also played a part in the religious disputes that were rife in Antwerp at that time. During the night of 15 August 1566 the Calvinists built a pulpit against one of the end walls where the pastor, Hendrik Modet, wanted to preach a sermon. William of Orange, fearful of a confrontation with Spain, advised him against it. Modet obeyed, but less than a month later the Protestants constructed a clandestine chapel out of a cowshed on the Hesseplein. During the Protestant regime in Antwerp the Lutherans acquired their own church on the first floor of the Hessen House. Here on 22 July 1580 Archduke Mathias resigned as governor general of the 17 United Provinces in the presence of the States-General. Archduke Mathias did not want to become entangled in the religious and political chaos of the time and left for Germany, where he was to become emperor several years later. In the Hessen House he warned the rebellious Dutch one last time about the wrath of the Spain which was now threatened: 'I give back to you all that you have entrusted to me by your oath of loyalty to authorities and government – make use of it, but know that you shall have to account to God and the king for your deeds.'

✚ 30B4
✉ Falconrui 53
☎ 03–2060350
🕐 Tue–Sun 10–5
🍴 Excellent cafés (£–££) and restaurants (£–£££) in the area
🚊 4, 7
🚌 9, 6/34
♿ Good
💲 Cheap
↔ Berg van Barmhartigheid (➤ 32), Prinsenhof (➤ 59), Stadswaag (➤ 66)

Hessenhuis, silent witness of several high points of the religious disputes in Antwerp

HUIS VAN ROOSMALEN ⭐

With this corner house the architect van Reeth in 1985 set a new trend in the architecture on the wharves. The house is a reminder of the world of shipping, on the other side of the quays. The black-and-white pattern is also a nod towards a house that the Austrian architect Adolf Loos designed for the singer Josephine Baker – however, that design was never realised.

HORTIFLORA (➤ 110)

INSTITUUT VOOR TROPISCHE GENEESKUNDE ⭐

This institute was set up in 1933 to prepare doctors for their work in the Belgian colonies. It is now an international establishment for academic research and post-graduate teaching in tropical medicine and nursing. The Institute of Tropical Medicine also has a role in the research into a cure for Aids. The facade and interior are sober art deco. The modern garden with wrought ironwork inspired by Africa is free and worth a visit.

INTERNATIONAAL ZEEMANSHUIS ⭐

When this modern building was opened in 1954 the city authorities had a clear aim in mind: 'to provide reasonable accommodation, care and relaxation for all foreign and Belgian seamen who were staying in the city'. It was rumoured that the Internationaal Zeemanshuis (International Seamen's House) had been built deliberately close to the old Schipperskwartier (➤ 63), the red-light district of Antwerp and the favourite centre of entertainment for the seamen. Apart from bedrooms the guests also have the use of a library, a reading room, a meeting room, a bar-cum-restaurant and a small theatre. Seamen do not stay here so much now because ships are usually turned round in less than a day, but the International Seamen's House is becoming more and more popular with truckers and tourists.

A Walk Along the Meir Shopping Street

Start at Centraal Station (➤ 19). Antwerp Zoo (➤ 26) is also close by. The instructions for this walk are very straightforward: simply keep straight on, heading for the Boerentoren skyscraper (➤ 33) in the distance.

From Centraal Station walk towards the Keyserlei and follow it through.

Shopping actually starts here. Keyserlei is a busy shopping street with several cafés and restaurants. Walk past the Gaumont Filmzalen (➤ 39).

Cross over Teniersplaats and enter Leysstraat (➤ 53). Follow this until it becomes the Meir, then keep straight on.

On sunny Saturdays thousands of people stroll down this wide shopping street. There is everything to see. There are of course the shops: nearly all the big chains have a branch in the street. In addition, street theatre and performances by mime artists add atmosphere and there are all kinds of information stands.

You will then pass the Osterriethuis (➤ 58) and further on the Koninklijk Paleis (➤ 51).

Halfway down the Meir you come to the square known as the Wapper with the Rubenshuis (➤ 23) on the left. You can have a drink or something to eat in one of the cafés here.

Follow the Meir until it becomes Meirbrug which ends at the Boerentoren. Turn left here along Schoenmarkt as far as Groenplaats where you could catch the Metro (➤ 121) back to Centraal Station.

Groenplaats (➤ 42) is very popular with both residents of Antwerp and tourists. You can see the statue of Rubens here (➤ 62).

Distance
1.5km

Time
1–2 hours

Start point
Centraal Station
✚ 31C3
🚊 2, 15

End point
Groenplaats

Lunch
Rubens Inn (££)
✉ Wapper 17
☎ 03–2263327

The fashionable Leysstraat looking towards Centraal Station

Opposite: *architecture of the 1980s inspired by shipping*

49

JORDAENSHUIS

🟦42A1
✉ Reyndersstraat 6
☎ 03–2010011 (Art Gallery)
🍴 Excellent cafés and
   restaurants in the area
🚊 2, 3, 4, 7, 8, 10, 11, 15
♿ Few
↔ Vlaeykensgang (➤ 67)

Between 1639 and 1641, when the painters Rubens and van Dyck seemed to be reaching the end of their lives, the painter Jacob Jordaens had this house built between the Reyndersstraat and the Hoogstraat, where he was born. Together with Rubens and van Dyck, Jordaens formed the 'baroque trio' but he was always somewhat under the shadow of the other two, a fact that he did not seem to find difficult. In contrast to van Dyck and Rubens, Jordaens

never left Antwerp except for a journey to Brussels or The Hague. He lacked the ambition and restlessness of van Dyck and for years worked with Rubens on, for example, the planning and painting of the *The Joyous Entry* of the Cardinal-Infante Ferdinand of Austria. When Rubens died, Jordaens did not feel it beneath him to finish off the Rubens paintings for the Tore de la Parada in Madrid ordered by King Philip IV. In 1616 Jordaens married Catherine, the daughter of his teacher, the Protestant Adam van Noort. Late in life Jordaens converted to Calvinism and even that scarcely damaged his career. Nowadays his house contains an art gallery and a shop.

KLOOSTERSTRAAT

🟦30A2
✉ Kloosterstraat
🍴 Excellent cafés and
   restaurants in the area
🚊 4, 8
↔ Instituut voor Tropische
   Geneeskunde (➤ 48)

Above: *the house of the painter Jacob Jordaens, now an art gallery*

Legend has it that the powerful St Michielsabdij (St Michael's Abbey) of the Premonstratensians that once stood here was founded after the invasion of the Vikings in 836. However that may be, during the Middle Ages the Premonstratensian abbey, as a complex of buildings, made its mark on the development of Antwerp. Its power was only broken by the Austrians in the 18th century. The art treasures of the abbey were looted under Napoleon Bonaparte, who installed his shipyards in the buildings. The deathblow came in direct connection with the riots during the Belgian revolution of 1830. William I had turned the abbey into a prison and depot and it contained an extensive arsenal. On 27 October 1830 the Belgian volunteers organised a raid on it to acquire the weapons. As a reaction General Chassé, commander of the south citadel, began the famous bombardment of the Kloosterstraat. When it was over, all that was left of the abbey was the tower, which was demolished in 1833. Today Kloosterstaat is outstanding as a centre for all kinds of shops selling antiques and bygones. Tourists can spend hours browsing about among antiques and trinkets old and new.

KONINKLIJK MUSEUM VOOR SCHONE KUNSTEN ✪✪✪

The Royal Museum of Fine Arts is one of the most imposing buildings in the city. It gives a good overview of art in the Low Countries from the 14th century. You can admire works by de Keyser in the impressive entrance hall. The upper floor houses works by old masters such as Jan van Eyck, Rogier van der Weyden, Hans Memling, Quinten Metsys, Brueghel the Elder and the Younger, Rubens, van Dyck, Jordaens and so on. The ground floor is devoted to the art of the 19th and 20th centuries: James Ensor, Constant Permeke, René Magritte, the Flemish Expressionists and the Experimentalists.

🏠 30B1
✉ Leopold De Waelplaats
☎ 03–2387809
🕐 Tue–Sun 10–5, Easter Monday and Whit Monday. Closed 1 Jan, 1 May, Ascension Day, 25 Dec
🍴 Excellent cafés and restaurants in the area
🚋 12, 24
♿ Good
💰 Moderate
↔ Zuiderpershuis (► 70)

KONINKLIJK PALEIS ✪

The Royal Palace was built in 1750 by Van Baurscheit and bought by Napoleon from the owner. It was later taken over by the Dutch rulers and the Belgian royal family used it as a residence. It now houses the International Cultural Centre and the Film Museum, with exhibitions and film showings.

🏠 30B3
✉ Meir 51
☎ 03–2248500
🍴 Excellent cafés (££) and restaurants (££) in the area
🚋 2, 3, 15
♿ Few
↔ Osterriethhuis (► 58), Rubenshuis (► 23), Vogelenmarkt (► 68)

Koninklijk Paleis on the Meir

KRUIDTUIN ✪✪✪

The herb garden is a place to escape from the hustle and bustle of the city. There used to be a school of medicine, chemistry and botany next to the St Elisabethziekenhuis (St Elisabeth Hospital) and the plants were grown in this garden. Now it is a botanic garden and you can enjoy the peace and quiet among remarkable trees, flowers, herbs and shrubs.

🏠 30B2
✉ Leopoldstraat
🕐 8–5:45
🍴 Excellent cafés and restaurants in the area
🚋 7, 8
♿ Few

Lambermontplaats, also known as 'le petit Paris'

LAMBERMONTPLAATS ✪

Once upon a time this square with its lovely, three-storey prosperous residences with white-plastered frame gables was called 'le petit Paris'. In the centre of the square there is a sculpture of a ship, an ode to the great expansion of Antwerp as a port in the 19th century. And if you look through the Waterpoort (► 70) you can sometimes see a ship sailing by on the Scheldt.

🚩 30A1
✉ Lambermontplaats
🍴 Excellent cafés (££) and restaurants (££) in the area
🚌 8, 12
↔ Waterpoort (► 70)

LEYSSTRAAT ✪

Leysstraat was laid out at the end of the 19th century when the 16th-century Spanish walls, now the Leien, were demolished. Leysstraat links the old Meir with the new Keyserlei and Centraal Station and forms part of Antwerp's foremost shopping route. At the time neither money nor effort were spared to make the facades as impressive as possible. Antwerp wanted to show off its prosperity and the city planners designed a curve in the street to make the view even more impressive.

🚩 31C3
🍴 Excellent cafés (££) and restaurants (££) in the area
🚌 2, 11
↔ Centraal Station (► 19)

MAAGDENHUIS ✪✪✪

In 1553 a merchant opened a house here for 'poor young maids'. The Maagdenhuis (Girls' Home) amassed a whole series of works of art because at that time prosperous residents of Antwerp believed that they could buy their way to heaven through gifts in cash or kind. The orphanage moved in 1882 but the Maagdenhuis is still owned by the Public Centre for Social Welfare, though part of it is now a museum where the works of art donated at that time are on exhibition: paintings and sculptures but also furniture, stained-glass windows, bronzes and copper items. You will find here less well known works by Rubens and Jordaens, an early piece by van Dyck (*St Jerome*), and there is a beautiful Lady Chapel, originally connected with the medieval St Elisabethziekenhuis.

The old part of the hospital is now used as a cultural centre and conference venue. Concerts are organised here regularly.

🚩 30B2
✉ Lange Gasthuisstraat 33
☎ 03-2235620
🕐 Mon, Wed, Fri 10–5, Sat–Sun 1–5
🍴 Excellent cafés (££) and restaurants (££) in the area
🚌 7, 8
♿ Few
💲 Moderate
↔ Graanmarkt (► 40), Mayer van den Bergh Museum (► 54)

Left: detail of the impressive facades of the fashionable Leysstraat

Mayer van den Bergh Museum

Fritz Mayer van den Bergh (1858–1901) was an art connoisseur and a passionate collector. After his death his mother, Henriette van den Bergh, added to his collection. The results can now be admired in the museum named after him. The pride of the collection is the *Dulle Griet* by Pieter Brueghel the Elder, but Mayer van den Bergh also collected antique sculptures, illuminated manuscripts, coins, glass, carpets and furniture. The collection concentrates particularly on the 14th, 15th and 16th centuries, and it contains a unique collection of Gothic sculptures. In addition there are works by Quinten Metsys, Jan Mostaert, Joos van Cleve, Jan Brueghel, Pieter Aertsen and Cornelis Vos. There are also a number of medieval pieces including the 14th-century *Virgin and Child* by an unknown Bruges artist.

Middelheim Openluchtmuseum

Below right: antique camera from the collection of the Museum voor Fotografie

An open-air exhibition of sculpture held in 1950 was such a success that the then burgomaster, L. Craeybeckx, opened a permanent sculpture park here. Nearly 70 sculptures were too fragile to stand outside so they were housed in the Paviljoen Braem (Braem Pavilion). The park covers 12 hectares. The Openluchtmuseum (Open-air Museum) changes with the rhythm of the seasons, from stark grey under winter skies to sparkling colour under the bright summer sun.

The park enjoys an international reputation. All the main trends and names from sculpture are represented here, from Rodin to Zadkine and Moore, from classical images to hypermodern installations. You can find the older works in the part of the park known as Middelheim Hoog; the more recent works of art are in Middelheim Laag.

Museum voor Fotografie

The Museum of Photography is a provincial museum in the former Vlaanderen warehouse (1912). There are several sections in the museum: the history of photography, various photographic techniques, and the art of photography. The showpieces include a photo album from the Great Exhibition held in London in 1851, a portable dark-room, and an automatic stereo-scope from 1905.

MUSEUM VOOR HEDENDAAGSE KUNST ANTWERP (MUKHA) ✪✪✪

The Antwerp Museum of Contemporary Art exhibits its collection in a renovated grain silo and a new building. There is a wonderful view over the city from the cafeteria on the roof. The collection itself concentrates on visual arts since the 1970s and includes the collection of the Stichting Matta Clark (Matta Clark Foundation). Temporary exhibitions are arranged annually.

➕ Not on the map
📧 Leuvenstraat 43–47
☎ 03-2385960
🕐 Tue–Sun 10–5. Closed 1 Jan, 1 May, Ascension Day, 25 Dec
🍴 Good cafés (£–£££) and restaurants (£–£££)
🚋 12, 24, 8, 4
♿ Good 🚻 Moderate

NIEUWE GAANDERIJ ✪✪✪

This shopping arcade connects two busy shopping areas. In the stylish architecture of the 1950s you can find all kinds of boutiques for shoes, clothes, jewellery and so on. All the boutiques dating from the 1970s are on two floors.

➕ 30B3
📧 Huidevettersstraat 38, Korte Gasthuisstraat 21
🍴 Good cafés (£–£££) and restaurants (£–£££)
🚋 2, 3, 15 ♿ Few

ONZE-LIEVE-VROUWEKATHEDRAAL (► 21, TOP TEN)

The Opera House with impressive steps that lead to a beautiful interior staircase

OPERA ✪✪✪

The Vlaamse Opera (Flemish Opera, 1907, architect A. van Mechelen) is not seen to best advantage nowadays since project developers dumped the hideous Antwerp Tower beside it in the 1970s. Yet it remains a monument with an imposing staircase, a lovely marble interior and gilded plaster work. You can sample the atmosphere of grand opera and *soirées musicales*. In recent years the Flemish Opera has earned international acclaim for, according to connoisseurs, its adventurous performances. The cheaper seats are often booked up months in advance.

➕ 31C3
📧 Frankrijklei 3
☎ 03-2336808
🍴 Excellent cafés (£–£££) and restaurants (£–£££) in the area
🚌 All buses direction Rooseveltplaats
♿ Poor
🔄 Centraal Station (► 19)

Food & Drink

Belgians in general are very fond of food and drink, and the people of Antwerp perhaps especially so. The city has more than 600 restaurants and 1,800 cafés, many with open-air seating, where you can have a snack as well as something to drink. There is no official closing time in Antwerp, an evening out can extend into the small hours. And then of course it's time for breakfast at a pavement café.

The legendary Frituur No. 1 in the Hoogstraat in Antwerp

Food

Belgian cuisine is some of the best in Europe. In Antwerp you can find top restaurants that regularly carry off prestigious distinctions and prizes. Belgian cuisine is French in essence, with great attention paid to rich sauces and fresh ingredients. Residents of Antwerp expect much of their restaurants and have only contempt for pretentious menus or restaurants where the prices are too high. Their standard is simple but good food that is professionally prepared – otherwise they might just as well eat at home. Not only top restaurants conform to this standard, it applies equally to bars serving food or the fish-and-chip stand on the corner.

Sunday lunch can easily last for a couple of hours and even run on into coffee and cake in the afternoon.

Business restaurants specialise in serving excellent but reasonably priced lunches at top speed.

In addition to Belgian cuisine you can find a great variety of international restaurants in Antwerp. Chinese, Japanese, Persian, Moroccan, African, and others – you will find them all in this port city. Fierce competition ensures that the quality is usually more than excellent.

Traditional Belgian cuisine relies very heavily on meat dishes but most restaurants have at least two vegetarian

People in Antwerp enjoy their meals and they demand perfection

alternatives to fall back on. These are usually shown on the menu. If not, it is perfectly acceptable to ask for them.

Chocolate

Belgian chocalate is known all over the world. Belgians consume 7.8 kilos of chocolate per person annually. Buying chocolates in Antwerp is relatively cheap because of the high turnover.

When going visiting, people in Antwerp are just as likely to take a box of chocolates with them as a bunch of flowers. In the speciality shops it is always busy: staff wearing white gloves fill the boxes with the customer's choice or suggest a mixed box if someone is unable to make up his or her mind.

Antwerp's way of life includes visiting the many pleasant cafés

Beer

A hundred years ago there were more than 3,000 breweries in Belgium. Most have merged to form larger breweries so that nowadays there are no more than 120, producing some 500 varieties of beer. Together these produce an annual total of 14,000 million litres, or 1,000 litres per Belgian. Much of this is naturally destined for export although it does not always seem like it. A typical Antwerp beer is *Koninck*. A *bolleke Koninck*, or *bolleke* for short, is a brown beer that is poured into a tulip-shaped glass on a tall stem. To celebrate van Dyck year a new beer with a high alcohol content came on to the market: the *Antoon*. In the cafés of Antwerp you will also find a treasure house of other speciality and trappist beers.

Belgian breweries produce annually on average 1,000 litres of beer per inhabitant of the country

Trappist beers are no longer brewed by Cistercian monks – there are just too few of them – but monasteries supervise the brewing process. Trappist beers can be bought in bottles in the supermarkets all over Belgium but it is exported less than other types of Belgium beer such as Pils and Stella Artois. Most of the Trappist monasteries do not wish to increase production because they are afraid that the quality would suffer.

The Osterriethhuis on the Meir

🕂 30B3
✉ Meir 85
🍴 Excellent cafés
(£–£££) and restaurants
(£–£££) in the area
🚊 2, 3, 15
♿ Poor
↔ Rubenshuis (➤ 23),
Vogelenmarkt (➤ 68)

🕂 30B2
✉ Oudaan
🍴 Excellent cafés
(£–£££) and restaurants
(£–£££) in the area
🚊 7, 8
♿ Good
↔ Bourlaschouwburg
(➤ 33)

🕂 42A2
✉ Hofstraat 15
🍴 Excellent cafés
(£–£££) and restaurants
(£–£££) in the area
🚊 2, 15
↔ Groenplaats (➤ 42)

OSTERRIETHHUIS

In the 18th century, Antwerp had a prosperous German community which left traces behind. The Osterrieth family had a splendid rococo palace built which is now the headquarters of an international bank. The majestic staircase and inner courtyard are open to visitors. It is unfortunately not possible to see the bank's art collection, which contains many old and modern Flemish masters. The corner house on Eikenstraat is in fact an older building that was adapted to become the larger palace.

OUDAAN

This is the headquarters of the city police, and is known locally as 'the police tower'. A whole neighbourhood was demolished here in the 1950s, including a unique 19th-century shopping arcade. In its place a huge administrative complex was to have been built of which only this tower was ever erected. Love it or hate it, together with the Boerentoren (➤ 33) and Onze-Lieve-Vrouwekathedraal (➤ 21) the Oudaan determines the skyline of Antwerp. The police eat their lunch on the highest floor but one; they have a wonderful view of the whole city.

OUDE BEURS

This was not the first exchange in Antwerp: from 1353 traders used to meet in the house called 'De Borze', which was approximately on the corner of the Wisselstraat. But in 1515 they moved to this building. It is now the headquarters of the officials of the City Education Department. The Oude Beurs has a beautifully decorated gallery round a plain inner courtyard. In the corner there is a fine example of a late Gothic tower house (1616).

Below: *view of the attractive Pieter Potstraat*

PIETER POTSTRAAT (GROTE AND KLEINE) ✪✪

Pieter Pot was a rich banker from Utrecht who settled in Antwerp in 1604. You can sense the medieval atmosphere of these narrow streets, particularly in Kleine Pieter Potstraat. There are many restaurants and cafés in Grote Pieter Potstraat. A must for warm summer evenings.

🔳 42A1
✉ Pieter Potstraat (Grote and Kleine)
🍴 Excellent cafés (£–£££) and restaurants (£–£££) in the area
🚊 2, 15

PLANTIN MORETUS MUSEUM (➤ 22, TOP TEN)

PRINSENHOF ✪✪✪

The Prinsenhof is one of the hidden gems of Antwerp. At 70m the frontage is the longest in the city. It was built by the knight Arnold van Liere and Albrecht Dürer wrote about it in his travel diary: 'Such a splendid building have I never seen in all the German lands'. During his visit to Antwerp in 1520 Prince Charles, later Emperor Charles V, chose to stay here, rather than in the other Prinsenhof, which belonged to the St Michielsabdij in Kloosterstraat (➤ 50). At the time this could have caused an incident, but the Prinsenhof and Prinsenstraat, where it stands, adopted their names temporarily.

After van Liere died, his heirs sold the Prinsenhof to the city of Antwerp. It granted right of use to the Italian merchant family Salviati, and later the house was occupied by the British governor together with English wool merchants. The Prinsenhof changed its name to 'Engelsch Huys'. The Engelsch Huys survived the rampage known as the Spanish Fury and in 1607 was transformed by the Jesuits into a school for the study of philosophy and theology; from then on it was referred to as the 'English Fathers'. The impressive quadrangles of the Prinsenhof even today bear comparison with those of an Oxford college.

The Jesuit order was disbanded in 1773, and the contents of the house were taken and sold publicly on the Vrijdagmarkt. It was only in 1929 that the Prinsenhof was again up for sale and the Jesuits were able to win back their old college. It now belongs to the University of Antwerp. The inner courtyards and galleries are open to visitors.

🔳 30B3
✉ Prinsstraat 13
🍴 Excellent cafés (£–££) and restaurants (£–££) in the area
🚊 4, 7
🚌 9, 6/34
♿ Good
↔ Archief en Museum van heth Vlaamse Cultuur-leven (➤ 32), Berg van Barmhartigheid (➤ 32), Stadswaag (➤ 66), Hessenhuis (➤ 47)

A Green Walk Round Middelheim Park

Distance
3km

Time
4–6 hours

Start point
⊕ 74A2
Floraliënlaan, on the corner
of Middelheimlaan
🚌 18, 27, 32

End point
Eglantierlaan
🚌 17, 18

Lunch
Take a picnic with you

Middelheim Openlucht-museum is an open-air museum with a vast collection of more than 300 sculptures

It is a good idea to take lunch with you on this walk. Leave from the Floraliënlaan.

Turn left into Middelheimlaan and follow this until you reach Beukenlaan and then turn right.

You then come to the Middelheim Openluchtmuseum (► 54), an open-air sculpture museum which is well worth a visit. Sometimes the statues seem to be part of their green surroundings, sometimes they form a contrast. Locals like to come here just to walk, have a picnic, go jogging or simply laze on the grass. Children and parents enjoy picnicking here.

Follow Beukenlaan to Acacialaan where you turn left.

First of all walk along amongst the greenery. Kasteel den Brandt (► 13) is on the left and the Hortiflora (► 13, 110) on the right with the Rubenstuin (► 13). Acacialaan gives the impression of a residential suburb of the city. Most of the houses were built after World War I. They include English-style cottages as well as gems of modern architecture. Cottage Sunlight (Acacialaan 33) is very pretty.

In Acacialaan, turn right into Seringenlaan and then immediately right again which brings you into Eglantierlaan. Walk towards the bus stop where you can catch the bus back to Antwerp or No. 18 to the Floraliënlaan.

ROCKOXHUIS ✪✪✪

A museum with a wealth of works of art from the baroque era. The museum is named after one of the most famous inhabitants of this 17th-century aristocrat's house, Nicolaas Rockox. Nicolaas Rockox was the first burgomaster of Antwerp, a friend of Rubens and one of his most important clients. Rubens wrote of him: 'a fair man and a connoisseur of antiquities. He is wealthy, a good administrator, a gentleman with the most honourable reputation'. Apart from being a politician Rockox was also a scholar, an expert on coins, a bibliophile, an art specialist and a great collector. The painting *Samson and Delilah* by Rubens hung above the fireplace in his house. After Rockox's death, the house changed hands a number of times until it was bought in 1970 by a Belgian bank, together with the adjoining Snyderhuis, and turned into a museum. The exhibits include works by Rubens, van Dyck, Jordaens, Teniers, Brueghel and Metsys. Here you can see a study for the head of Jerome by van Dyck. The head can be found in two major works of van Dyck, one now in the Museum Boymans van Beuningen in Rotterdam and the other in the collection of the Prince of Lichtenstein in Vaduz.

RUBENSHUIS (➤ 23, TOP TEN)

➕ 30B3
✉ Keizerstraat 12
☎ 03–2314710
🕐 Tue–Sun 10–4:45, Easter Monday and Whit Monday. Closed 1–2 Jan, 1 May, Ascension Day, 1–2 Nov, 25–26 Dec
🍴 Excellent cafés (£–££) and restaurants (£–££) in the area
🚊 4, 7 🚌 9, 6/34
♿ Good
💲 Moderate
🔁 Berg van Barmhartigheid (➤ 32), Hessenhuis (➤ 47), Prinsenhof (➤ 59), Stadswaag (➤ 66)

Rockoxhuis belonged to Nicolaas Rockox, the first burgomaster of Antwerp

42B1

Groenplaats

Free

Excellent cafés and restaurants (£–£££) in the area

2, 15

Onze-Lieve-Vrouwe-Kathedraal (► 21)

RUBENS STATUE ★★★

The unveiling of the statue of the painter Pieter Paul Rubens did not take place without a struggle. In 1836 the city of Antwerp realised that the two hundredth anniversary of the great painter's death would occur in 1840 and that there was no monument to him anywhere in Antwerp. A Rubens committee was set up in haste and a search made for a sculptor. The sculptor Willem Geefs made the mould and Master Buckens from Luik was going to cast it. The Rubens committee had chosen a site in the Burchtplein (disappeared 1886) close to the Steen (► 25): 'looking out over the Scheldt and greeting the seafarers'. In August 1840 the statue was still not finished. To have something to unveil, a gilded plaster statue was made but it was broken on the journey to Antwerp. Willem Geefs produced a second, rejected example from his studio so that the plinth near the Steen would not remain empty. This temporary image stood there for a year, according to eyewitnesses damaged and smeared with garbage. The Rubens committee did not survive the fiasco; financially it was a great blow. In 1843 the committee finally handed over the original – finished – statue to the city of Antwerp in exchange for the settlement of their debts. The city decided to erect it in Groenplaats (► 42). The statue, weighing 15 tonnes, again rolled off its transport during the journey, but survived the fall. The writer Hendrik Conscience (► 14) gave an address at the unveiling, in which he expressed his relief that everything had, finally, turned out well.

The statue of Rubens, with Onze-lieve-Vrouwekathedraal in the background

*Side view of the
St Andrieskerk*

ST ANDRIESKERK

In the 16th century, the parish church of St Andrew formed part of the Augustinian monastery and through this it has links with a particular piece of history from the beginning of the Reformation. The German Augustinian canons were not entirely welcome when they founded a monastery in Antwerp in 1511; the Order of Onze-Lieve-Vrouw (Our Lady) in particular was opposed to them. In 1519 a number of Augustinian canons declared themselves in agreement with Luther's theses – he was himself an Augustinian – and the whole order soon followed. They were expelled violently from Antwerp, and two canons ended up being burnt at the stake by way of example. The Augustinians continued to preach in the open air and the city saw the need to close the church and sell the contents in public. Plantin acquired a beautiful example of the Gutenberg Bible for his collection. Services are still held in the church but it is now also a museum. The showpiece is an impressive 19th-century pulpit, although there are also various works of art by Flemish masters.

🔲 30A2
✉ St Andriesstraat 5
☎ 03–2320384
🕐 May–Sep: 2–5, except during services
🍴 Excellent cafés (£–££) and restaurants (£–££) in the area
🚊 4, 8
♿ Good
🎫 Cheap
↔ Plantin Moretus Museum (► 22)

SCHIPPERSKWARTIER

The Seamen's Quarter is the traditional red-light district of Antwerp, with its roots going back to the Middle Ages. There used to be a gallows field here. It later became a suburb of the city where seamen, dockworkers' families and prostitutes lived. After the second expansion of the city (1249–50), the Schipperskwartier came within the city boundary but it retained its rough character. Nowadays the area is known for window prostitution. What is less well known is that it has a number of outstanding cafés and discos.

🔲 30A4
✉ Veemarkt and surrounding streets
🕐 Free
🍴 Excellent cafés and restaurants (£–£££) in the area
🚊 4, 7 ♿ None
↔ Internationaal Zeemanshuis (► 48), St Pauluskerk (► 18)

In the Know

If you only have a short time to visit Antwerp and would like to get a real flavour of the city, here are some ideas:

A street musician at a pavement café in Groenplaats

Stroll along the wharves beside the Scheldt and let the wind blow through your hair.

Tell foreigners that Dutch is a variant of Standard Antwerps.

10
Ways to Be a Local

You can't be a *sinjoor* unless you were born in Antwerp and both your parents were local. People born in Antwerp whose parents came from elsewhere are known as *pagadders*.

Men should grow a moustache.

If you trip over the kerb write an angry letter to the official responsible and copy it to the burgomaster and the chief of police.

Spend the whole day chatting to complete strangers. Antwerp is the small talk capital of the world.

If the sun is shining: have a *bolleke Koninck* (pronounced 'kernink') at a pavement café.

If the sun isn't shining: have a *bolleke Koninck* in one of the heated terraces on the Grote Markt.

When driving: make frequent use of the horn to show other drivers what you think of their driving.

Complain that the city used to look nicer but never say that Antwerp is ugly. Agree with the person you are talking to that it won't be long before all the nice things have disappeared.

10
Top Lunch Places

Amadeus ££
✉ Jan Blomstraat 3–5
☎ 03–2340320 ◐
Tue–Sun 9:30–7.
Popular tearoom, ice-cream parlour and bar serving food. Speciality: jumbo mussels.

Antoon van Dyck £
✉ Grote Markt 4
☎ 03–2313565 ◐
Tue–Sun lunch and dinner. A tearoom, ice-cream parlour and restaurant in the painter's birthplace.

Modern architecture on Jordaenskaai

Bistro Royal, den Echte ££
✉ Veemarkt 27
☎ 03–2328580
🕐 Wed–Mon lunch and dinner.
Popular restaurant with 'political satirical' menu.

Den Blauwe Canard £
✉ Ossenmarkt 28
☎ 03–2324901
🕐 Mon–Sat lunch and dinner.
Specialities: duck, goose and foie gras. A light interior and a toaster on each table for toast with the foie gras.

't Brantijser ££
✉ Hendrik Conscienceplein 7
☎ 03–2331833 🕐 Daily lunch and dinner.
Pub with snacks and summery salads in 16th-century building in Antwerp's most attractive square.

Celtic Ireland £
✉ Groenplaats 1
☎ 03–2131450
🕐 Breakfast, lunch and dinner.
Atmospheric Irish café where you can enjoy Irish stew with Irish folk music in the background.

't Elfde Gebod ££
✉ Torfbrug 10
☎ 03–2893466
🕐 Daily lunch and dinner.
Romantic brasserie behind a medieval facade, famous for the statues of saints ranged around the dining room.

Haddock ££
✉ Amerikalei 8
☎ 03–2377801 🕐 Mon–Fri lunch and dinner, Sat–Sun dinner.
Local pub for people from the Law Courts. Many about to be sentenced drank their last glass in freedom here.

Milano £££
✉ Statiestraat 11
☎ 03–2326743
🕐 Thu–Tue lunch and dinner.
The best Italian cuisine. The restaurant is designed as an aristocrat's house. In the open kitchen you can see for yourself how the chef prepares your osso bucco.

Zuiderterras ££
✉ Ernest Van Dijckkaai 37
☎ 03–2341275
🕐 Breakfast, lunch and dinner.
Designed in the shape of a ship by the architect van Reeth. Classical to modern menu and a wonderful view across the Scheldt.

10
Things to Do

Museums: Antwerp has wonderful world-class museums. Take your time.
The Scheldt: walk along the quay or take a boat trip.
Walk: the best way to see Antwerp is on foot. Take comfortable shoes.
Stroll: strolling down the Meir is a favourite occupation in Antwerp. You can also shop there.
Architecture: few disasters left Antwerp untouched but you can still find beautiful buildings everywhere in the city, from the 15th century to the present day.
Art: you can find established art in the museums, new works in the galleries in the Antwerp South district.
Shop: Antwerp is the shopping city par excellence. You may find

The flea market on St. Jansvliet

your credit card begins to feel the strain!
Food: eat at a different restaurant or bar every day.
Drink: visit a different café or pub every day.
Music and dancing: enjoy the street theatre by Onze-Lieve-Vrouwekathedraal.

10
Beautiful Buildings

30A3
St Jansvliet
Excellent cafés (£–££) and restaurants (£–££) in the area
2, 3, 15
Poor
Free
Jordaenshuis (➤ 50), Vlaeykensgang (➤ 67)

30B4
Excellent cafés (£–££) and restaurants (£–££) in the area
4, 7
9, 6/34
Good
Moderate
Berg van Barmhartigheid (➤ 32), Prinsenhof (➤ 59), Hessenhuis (➤ 47)

ST ANNATUNNEL

The pedestrian tunnel under the Scheldt starts in the middle of St Jansvliet. There is a choice between using the wooden escalators or the art-deco lift to go down to the start of a white tunnel for the short walk (572m) under the river. Once on the other side you are rewarded by a splendid view of the wharves of Antwerp from the Linkeroever (left bank). Since the 1950s the city has been trying, with only limited success, to move the 'natural boundary' of Antwerp by opening up the left bank as a residential area.

ST JACOBSKERK (➤ 24, TOP TEN)

STADSWAAG

In 1548 Gilbert van Schoonbeke had the city weigh-house built here. The goods on sale by the merchants were not only weighed but also stored here, so the weigh-house was a large building and, to kill two birds with one stone, van Schoonbeke fitted out the upper floor as a reception room for wedding parties. This room later became the *chirugynskamer* (surgeon's room) used for courses in surgery and medicine. In 1797 the French occupying forces set up a polling booth here where the inhabitants could choose their representatives, but 20 years later the building was sold by the city. It became a storage

area and on 25 August 1873 the whole place was gutted by fire. The Stadswaag then became just an open space. Since the 1960s it has been a centre for popular culture, with jazz cafés and experimental theatre. Plans for an underground car park had to be shelved when the foundations of the old weigh-house were discovered under the building.

Stadswaag, a pleasant little square with several trendy cafés

THE STEEN (► 25, TOP TEN)

STUDIO HERMAN TEIRLINCK ✪
In this aristocrat's house aspiring actors and actresses undergo drama training in the school named after the writer and founder. In the famous pub opposite, Den Boer van Tienen, you might be lucky enough to spot some famous actors.

✚ Not on the map
✉ Maarschalk Gérardstraat 4
🍴 Excellent cafés (£–££) and restaurants (£–££) in the area ☕ 7, 8
↔ Maagdenhuis (► 53)

VAN WESEBEKESTRAAT ✪
A little piece of Chinatown in Antwerp. This is the shopping street for the Chinese community with provision stores, restaurants, hairdressers, travel agents and video shops. Belgians of Chinese origin come here from all over the country to stock up. Locals buy exotic products here and fireworks for New Year celebrations.

✚ 31C3
🍴 Excellent cafés (£–££) and restaurants (£–££) in the area
☕ 2, 15, 11
♿ None
↔ Centraal Station (► 19)

Vlaeykensgang, a 16th-century alleyway and a peaceful oasis in the heart of Antwerp

VLAEYKENSGANG ✪✪✪
This is a tourist success: an inconspicuous gateway leads to a 16th-century alleyway, originally occupied by shoemakers. No one knows why it was called Vlaeykensgang. It is possible that it once contained a tart shop (Flemish *vlaaienhuis*). It was almost broken up in the 1960s because it had become so dilapidated. Fortunately that did not happen. There are several excellent restaurants and in the summer you can always hear the carillon concert from the nearby Onze-Lieve-Vrouwekathedraal (► 21).

✚ 30A3
✉ Oude Koornmarkt 16
🍴 Excellent cafés (£–££) and restaurants (£–££) in the area
☕ 2, 3, 4, 7, 8, 10, 11, 15
♿ Few
↔ Jordaenshuis (► 50), St Annatunnel (► 66)

67

➕ 42A2
✉ Vleeshouwersstraat
   38–40
☎ 03-2336404
🕐 Tue–Sun 10–4:45, Easter
   Monday and Whit
   Monday. Closed 1–2 Jan,
   1 May, Ascension Day,
   1–2 Nov, 25–26 Dec
🍴 Excellent cafés (£–££)
   and restaurants (£–££)
   in the area
🚌 2, 3, 15
♿ Few
↔ Hendrik Conscienceplein
   (➤ 46)

The Vogelenmarkt, on Sunday morning is a magnet for locals who do their shopping there and for tourists who want to enjoy watching it all

➕ 30B2
✉ Theaterplein and
   surrounding streets
🕐 Sunday morning
🍴 Excellent cafés (£–££)
   and restaurants (£–££)
   in the area
🚌 2, 3, 15
♿ None
↔ Osterriethhuis (➤ 58),
   Rubenshuis (➤ 23)

VLEESHUIS ✪✪✪

Master Herman de Waghemaekere was commissioned by the powerful butchers' guild to build this Late-Gothic guild house between 1502 and 1503. His butcher clients gave precise instructions: there had to be space to set up 62 stalls, the architect must provide a chapel, and it must be a splendid building because the neighbourhood had a bad name and they wanted to do something about it. At the time butchers were prohibited from setting up in business except in Vleeshouwersstraat, Kuipersstraat or Braderijstraat. There was a tension between the butchers' guild in Antwerp and the butchers of Borgerhout who, until the guilds were closed down often tried to smuggle their meat into the city. But in the 16th century a butcher who had one of the 62 stalls had become very prosperous. He was still forbidden to marry outside the guild.

The Vleeshuis is now a museum. It gives a lively impression of life in Antwerp at that time. The showpiece of the collection is a set of cymbals from the world-famous Ruckers workshop. As well as musical instruments, the museum has displays of metalwork, wood-carving and miscellaneous works of art and craft.

VOGELENMARKT ✪✪✪

This was a market where, from the 16th century, ducks, geese, snipe, wildfowl, herons, pigeons and small birds were sold for the table just as meat was sold in the Vleeshuis (➤ 68) and fish in the Vismarkt by the Steen (➤ 25). You can still buy poultry in this market. In addition you will also discover a bit of genuine Antwerp: stallholders who advertise their wares at the tops of their voices, buyers who try to beat them down.

For a number of years the sale of small pets, cats and dogs from market stalls has been prohibited, but they are still sold at the various pet shops round Vogelenmarkt.

VOLKSKUNDEMUSEUM ✪✪✪

Gildekamerstraat consists of a series of carefully restored historic buildings. These were originally guild houses. In 1936 there were plans to demolish them and erect a glass office block but fortunately this was never done. Behind these facades there is now a museum which gives an amazing picture of the folk culture of Antwerp and Flanders. The museum contains household items, and delves into recreation, religion and medicine. Striking features are a former apothecary's shop and the 18th-century alchemist's study.

VRIJDAGMARKT ✪✪

This was another project by the 16th-century developer Gilbert van Schoonbeke. He wanted to move the sellers of second-hand goods off Grote Markt (➤ 16) and this he managed to do. Since 1549 a traditional second-hand market has been held in the square every Friday (and Wednesday) and the goods belonging to bankrupts used to be sold here by auction. Vrijdagmarkt was reduced to rubble on 2 January 1945 by a German flying bomb. The square was rebuilt including a modern Catherine, patron saint of clothes-sellers, who gazes down from her plinth at the haggling going on at her feet. Miraculously the gable of the Plantin Moretus Museum (➤ 22) survived the attack.

✚ 42A2
⊠ Gildekamerstraat 2–6
☎ 03–2208653
🕐 Tue–Sun 10–4:45, Easter Monday and Whit Monday. Closed 1–2 Jan, 1 May, Ascension Day, 1–2 Nov, 25–26 Dec
🍴 Cafés and restaurants
🚊 2, 11, 15 ♿ Few
👤 Few
↔ Grote Markt (➤ 16), Stadhuis (➤ 16)

✚ 42A1
🍴 Excellent cafés (£–££) and restaurants (£–££)
🚊 4, 7, 8 ♿ Few
↔ Plantin-Moretus Museum (➤ 22)

Above: *view of a sun-drenched Vrijdagmarkt. This square was demolished during the war by a German flying bomb but has been rebuilt*

69

Waterpoort on the Gillisplaats, a triumphal arch in honour of the Prince Philip IV of Spain

30A1
Gillisplaats
Cafés (£–££) and restaurants (£–££) in the area
8, 12, 24
Lambermontplaats (► 53)

30A2
Hoek Waalse Kaai-Timmerwerfstraat
03–2487077
Excellent cafés and restaurants in the area
12, 24
Few   Moderate
Koninklijk Museum voor Schone Kunsten (► 51)

WATERPOORT   ✪✪

A 17th-century triumphal arch that has twice been moved: once from the Vlasmarkt to St Jansvliet and now to 't Zuid. The arch was intended as a tribute to the Spanish prince Philip IV. The design would have been done by Rubens.

ZOO (► 26, TOP TEN)

ZUIDERPERSHUIS   ✪✪

The oldest power station in the city. Water was collected in the two towers and put under pressure. An underground network allowed bridges, locks and harbour cranes to be worked by hydraulic power. The Zuiderpershuis is now a cultural centre for theatre, music and other stage arts, often from non-western cultures. Zuiderpershuis also has a popular bar serving food. At lunchtime the staff serve exotic snacks for office staff from the neighbourhood. In the summer you can eat in the inner courtyard.

ZWARTE PANTER GALERIJ ✪

The former St Julianusgasthuis, founded in 1303 by Ida van Der List and Johannes Tuclant, is one of the oldest charitable institutions in the city. Poor travellers could have a bed here for three nights. Until 1988 there was a rest home in the building, run by the Public Centre for Social Welfare as a women's refuge. It was, however, closed because of concerns over the fire risk and the building was let to the person who ran the Zwarte Panter (Black Panther) Gallery. Well-known contemporary painters in Antwerp such as Fred Bervoets and Jan Cox have had exhibitions here. The gallery is open to the public without charge.

➕ Not on the map
✉ Hoogstraat 70–72
☎ 03-2331345
🕐 Thu–Sun 2–6
🍴 Excellent cafés (£–££) and restaurants (£–££) in the area
🚋 2, 15
♿ Few
🎫 Free
↔ Groenplaats (➤ 42)

DID YOU KNOW?

Monks no longer live in the St Julianusgasthuis, but on Maundy Thursday each year a traditional pilgrim's meal is still organised in the chapel.

The Zwarte Panter Gallery, the former St Julianusgasthuis

Excursions from the City

Antwerp is a lovely city but there are all kinds of things to see in nearby places. For example, 30km south there is the historic town of Mechelen, once capital of The Netherlands and now a pleasant provincial town with beautiful treasures from its rich past. The area round Antwerp also has a fascinating history. Herentals was the flashpoint of the Boerenkring in the 18th century, a revolt against the French occupiers (► 77). From the tourist tower you get a wonderful view over the woods of Kempen; this was where the farmers hid during the revolt. In Geel a unique therapeutic experiment, running for centuries, is being followed with great interest by researchers from all over the world. And Lier was the home of the Flemish writer Felix Timmermans, creator of Pallieter, the archetype of the Flemish bon vivant. At the end of the book Pallieter withdraws into the 'wide, beautiful world, like the birds and the wind'. Even Pallieter could not resist the Kempen.

> *‘You must not be surprised that there is something of Rubens in these folk, because there was something of these folk in Rubens.’*

FELIX TIMMERMANS

———————•———————

Left: *St Romboutstoren towers above the Grote Markt in Mechelen*

🔲 74C1

Geel

Geel is dominated by Saint Dimpna and the 'idiots of Geel'. According to legend Dimpna was the daughter of an Irish king who lived at the end of the 7th or the beginning of the 8th century. Her father was a pagan but her mother had the child baptised and brought up in the Christian faith by the priest Gerebernus. When her mother died the king became mad with grief and wanted to marry his daughter who had inherited the beauty of her mother. Naturally this conflicted with the new faith of the young Dimpna so she fled from her father to Geel accompanied by the priest Gerebernus who had brought her up. After a long search her father found them and in a frenzy of despair and madness beheaded them both. Ever since then Geel has been a place of pilgrimage for those suffering from mental illness.

The story has had consequences: all the mentally ill who flocked to Geel could not be accommodated in the church's infirmary, so the custom developed of families taking one or more patients into their homes for a longer or shorter period. This kind of care existed from the Middle Ages and in 1850 the state formally recognised it. Nowadays researchers from all over the world study the 'Geel model' of care and integration.

Geel is a pleasant provincial town where it is nice to spend some time. There is a shopping street in the centre as well as numerous good eating places.

BAKKERIJMUSEUM DE WORFTHOEVE
In this bakery museum, you can see old waffle irons, icing moulds and moulds for chocolate, marzipan and gingerbread, griddles for baking communion wafers and much more, all in an old farmhouse. In the barn there is a collection of wagons and carts that were used in transport to and from the bakery.

☒ Worfthoeven 5
☎ 014–570950 (tourist office)
🕐 Apr–Oct: Sun 1–6. For groups by arrangement
🚉 Geel Station
♿ Few

ST AMANDSKERK
The present building, consecrated in 1532, replaced the previous one which was destroyed by fire in 1488 leaving only the tower. The tower is thus 14th century. The church is built of pink brick, white sandstone and brown ironstone. In times of unrest the town council would meet in a room directly under the tower, known as the aldermen's chamber. The interior of the church is largely baroque, with a pulpit dating from 1734 and an equally ornate high altar. The church also contains an 18th century sculpture group of the apostles, St Mary and the child Jesus with St Dimpna and her confessor Gerebernus (➤ 74). Armand Preud'homme once played the baroque organ of the church. He was organist there and resident in Geel from 1828 to 1941; he composed such Flemish evergreens as *Kempenland* and *In the Purple Heather* during his time there.

☒ Grote Markt
☎ 014–570950 (tourist office)
🕐 Tue 10–12, Sat 3–5
🍴 Excellent cafés and restaurants in the area
🚉 Geel Station
♿ Few

St Armandskerk in Geel

✉ Gasthuisstraat
☎ 014-570950 (tourist office)
🕐 Mon–Fri 9–4
🍴 Excellent cafés and restaurants in the area
🚉 Geel Station
♿ Few

ST DIMPNAKERK ✪✪✪

There was already a church here in the 8th century dedicated to St Martin. When the veneration of St Dimpna increased, the parish church of St Martin was replaced by the St Dimpna Church. The nave and side aisles date from 1349 and were built in Demer Gothic, a style typical of the areas of South Kempen and Hageland, with characteristics such as the use of ironstone and the lack of capitals to the pillars. It is therefore very plain. The transept, choir and choir aisle were later additions, together with the red-brick tower (1560). Adjoining the tower is the famous infirmary in which patients with mental afflictions could take refuge. In 1944 the infirmary of 1663 was destroyed but it has since been rebuilt.

✉ Gasthuisstraat 1
☎ 014-591443
🕐 Tue–Fri and Sun 2–5:30. Closed on feast days
🍴 Excellent cafés and restaurants in the area
🚉 Geel Station
♿ Few

ST DIMPNA EN GASTHUISMUSEUM ✪✪

You have already read about the legend of the holy Dimpna (➤ 74). Geel became a popular place of pilgrimage where people came to ask the help of St Dimpna in cases of mental illness. In 1270 Geel already had a hospice where poor sufferers could be treated without charge and if need be provided with accommodation. In 1552 Jan de Merode, lord of Geel, asked the Augustinian canonesses to take over the provision of this care. Apart from the excellent free care of the poor, the sisters also looked after paying patients. As a result they were able to build a whole complex and be self sufficient. The St Dimpna and Hospice Museum consists of a series of 17th-, 18th- and 19th-century buildings, and the complex includes three wards that you can visit, a bakery, butcher, laundry, servants' kitchen, the patients' chapel and the convent chapel. The buildings and equipment give a good idea of daily life at that time. The museum also houses a number of works of art from churches and chapels in Geel. The farmhouse has a pleasant bar where you can have a drink after your visit.

The Hospice Museum gives a good impression of the care of the mentally ill in Geel

✉ Gasthuisstraat 1
☎ 014-591443
🕐 Tue–Fri and Sun 2–5:30. Closed on feast days
🍴 Excellent cafés and restaurants in the area
🚉 Geel Station
♿ Few

ST DIMPNAKAPEL ✪

According to legend the holy Dimpna and the priest Gerebernus lived here in a hut close to the chapel until Dimpna's father found them. The chapel itself dates from the 17th century; it replaced a smaller chapel and was restored for the first time in 1780. Inside there is a lovely plain altar dated 1711. Near the chapel there is an even older well and a 350-year-old lime tree.

Herentals

Herentals is a charming little town with a wealth of historic monuments. It is particularly famous as the former capital of Kempen and the place where the Boerenkring was defeated. The Boerenkring (1796–98) was an uprising of farmers' sons against the French occupying power that wanted to conscript them into the army. The leader of the farmers' revolt was the advocate L. J. Heylen of Herentals and in the streets of the town the conflict finally ended with the French being victorious. There is a monument to the Boerenkring on the Grote Markt.

LAKENHAL ✪✪

The Cloth Hall, the former town hall on the Grote Markt, was rebuilt in 1534 after a devastating fire. Documents mention a building from 1430 onwards. In the rebuilding of 1534 a 35m-high octagonal bell tower was added. In 1541 the tower had a carillon and concerts still take place here every summer (each Friday in July and August, 21–22). There is a bell on a plinth in front of the town hall which is a reminder of the Eighty Years War in the 16th century. The armies involved were looting all bells to melt them down for cannons, and to avoid this the town council hung the clock in the bell tower. The tower was too light for the 800kg weight so the bell ended up on a plinth in front of the town hall.

The town hall now houses the Fraikin Museum. Fraikin was an apothecary in Herentals who in 1880 decided to become a sculptor. Three years before he died he donated a number of sculptures to the town. Those that are on display in the town hall are too big or too heavy to move, and Fraiken himself probably mounted them *in situ*. His other sculptures are being stored at a military depot until they find a permanent home, which is likely to be in the nearby Le Peige castle.

TOERISTENTOREN ✪✪

Gives a wonderful view of the Kempen countryside, a large area of woods, heath, dunes and moorland. The tower itself is 24m high and stands at the highest point in Herentals, 40m above sea level. You can wander for hours through the woods near the tower.

✚ 74B2

✉ Grote Markt
☎ 014–219088
🕐 Mon–Fri 9–5
🍴 Excellent cafés and restaurants in the area
🚉 Herentals Station
♿ Few

Above: the Cloth Hall in Herentals

✉ Along the main road in the direction of Lichtaart
🕐 Tower is open to visitors
🚉 Difficult to reach except by car
♿ None

77

Right: *the pleasant almshouses (Begijnhof) of Hoogstraten*

🔲 74B2

Hoogstraten

Hoogstraten is an extremely attractive small town on the Dutch border. Little is known about its origins; but according to legend the Norman Gemel built a castle in the neighbourhood. However that may be, Hoogstraten was mentioned for the first time in 1210 in a document of Duke Henry I of Brabant. Hoogstraten already had the privileges of a town – a town so small it is impossible to get lost. All the things worth seeing are close together.

BEGIJNHOF ✪✪

This walled village actually consists of two parts. According to deeds which have been discovered the older part was founded in 1380. In the 17th century a second part was built on. At the end of the 19th century the village housed 160 lay sisters living a modified form of the religious life. The last sister lived there until 1973, when the almshouses were almost lost through neglect. But then the present residents formed a non-profit-making organisation, called the Convent, and started a thorough restoration of the almshouses. In 1998 they were awarded the Henry Ford Conservation Award for this initiative.

GEMELSLOT ✪✪

The Gemelslot or Hoogstraten Castle would have been built in the 9th century by Gemel, the leader of the Normans. Yet the castle does not look rough or threatening. It was renovated and strengthened for the first time in the 16th century by the counts of Lalaing who went to live there. The castle had various functions after 1810: first it was a shelter for the homeless, then an agricultural home and later still a refuge.

Since 1931 the Gemeslot has been a school for young offenders. Young people who have been convicted of a criminal offence are given training to enable them to reintegrate into society.

🔲 Vrijheid
☎ 03–3401955 (tourist office)
🕐 Daily during the day, please respect the privacy of the residents
🍴 Excellent cafés and restaurants in the area
♿ Few

🔲 Lindendreef
☎ 03–3401955 (tourist office)
🕐 Can only be viewed from outside
🍴 Excellent cafés and restaurants in the area
♿ Few

Lier

Lier, 17km from Antwerp, is a pleasant, attractive provincial town with a long history. It stands at the confluence of the Grote and Kleine Nete rivers. There are traces of settlement back as far back as the times of the Romans and the Franks. In the 8th century St Gummarus, patron saint of the church which bears his name (► 81), would have played an important part in the development of the town, although his exact role is unclear. It is, however, known that after his death his body was brought to Lier from his birthplace of Emblem. A tradition of great devotion to the saint developed.

Romantic view of the sun-drenched Nete in Lier

The first record of *Ledi* (waterway) dates from 870. In 1212 the place received town status from Duke Henry I of Brabant. Various religious orders were established in Lier and helped the town to grow; in 1268 Sister Beatrijs wrote *Seven Manieren van Heiliger Minnen* (*Seven Ways of Love*), the oldest prose work in Middle Dutch, at the Cistercian abbey of Nazareth. Lier experienced its period of greatest prosperity between the 13th and 15th centuries thanks to the cloth industry and the cattle trade. The town had the opportunity to choose between cattle trade or a university as a reward for services rendered to Duke Jan II. The inhabitants chose their stomachs in preference to their heads and were nicknamed *schapenkoppen* (mutton heads). The rapid growth of Antwerp in the 15th century put an end to Lier's success. There was a revival two centuries later, again thanks to the cattle trade and a new industry, brewing. At any one time Lier had about 40 breweries. The Flemish writer Felix Timmermans lived and wrote there from 1886 to 1947 (► 82).

✚ 74B1

✉ Begijnhofstraat 25
☎ 03–4883888 (tourist office)
🕐 Unresticted, but please respect the privacy of the residents
🍴 Excellent cafés and restaurants in the area
🚉 Lier Station
♿ Few

Entrance to the alms-houses. St Begga gazes down from her niche at the entrance gate

✉ Florent van Cauwenberghstraat 14
☎ 03–4911396
🕐 Apr–Oct: Tue–Thu, Sat–Sun 10–12 and 1–15:30
🍴 Excellent cafés and restaurants in the area
🚉 Lier Station
♿ Good
💰 Moderate

BEGIJNHOF ●●●

This almshouse complex with 162 cottages and 11 cobbled streets actually forms a village within the town. It is very pleasant to wander past the houses which have a countrified look. Although the almshouses were founded in the 13th century, most of the houses you see are 17th century. They have wonderful names, such as *Wijngaerd des Heeren* (Lord's Vineyard), *'t Soete Naemken* (Sweet Name) and *Vijf Wondekens* (Five Wounds). Saint Begga gazes down on visitors from her niche above the entrance gate. The little gateway beside the main entrance was previously used as an emergency entrance at night, since at sunset all the other entrances to the almshouses were locked. The attractive St Margareta-kerk stands in the middle of the complex. It is in Flemish baroque with a rococo tower but is oversized in proportion to the village. The tower clock has only one hand, typical for the Middle Ages because time was reckoned in hours rather than minutes. St Margaretkerk is not open regularly. If it is open, it is well worth a look inside.

MUSEUM WUYTS ●●●

Town museum with a remarkable collection for a provincial establishment. It contains works by Jan Steen, Pieter Paul Rubens (► 14) and also by two of the three Brueghels, Jan and Pieter the Younger. The best-known work is *Flemish Proverbs* by Pieter Brueghel; the artist has included about 80 Flemish sayings. Brueghel saw the painting as a satire on human vice and folly. Each saying is noted (in Dutch) below its illustration.

A ticket for this museum includes entrance to the Timmermans-Opsomerhuis (► 82).

ST GUMMARUSKERK ✪✪

St Gummarus is the patron saint of marital problems. According to legend, St Gummarus, a member of the household of Pepin the Short, was married to Grimmara, an insufferable woman who made his life and that of their subjects a misery. The holy Gummarus did what men in that situation often do: he threw himself into his work and spent nine years away at the war with Pepin to keep order in the Frankish kingdom. When he returned he saw how in his absence Grimmara had taken out her wrath on the people of Lier. In despair Gummarus asked God to set her on the right path again and he promised in return to found a house of prayer. The St Gummarus church was built later, in the Brabant Gothic style. Construction took two centuries, from 1378 to 1517. The church treasure includes silver from the 17th, 18th and 19th centuries. The *Koningsramen* (Kings Windows) in the choir, made in 1516 by the then court glazier Nicolaas Rombouts, are the oldest existing windows to possess Renaissance characteristics in the whole of Flanders and The Netherlands. The church also possesses a shroud, though it is less well known than the Turin shroud. Two copies are extant; the other is kept at Xabregas near Lisbon. The shroud has a Latin text in Gothic script, stating that this shroud has the image of Christ after He was taken down from the cross and wrapped in the shroud by Joseph of Aramathea. There is, of course, serious doubt about whether the Lier shroud is the real shroud, but it remains very important as comparative material for research.

✉ Kardinaal Mercierplein
☎ 03–4883888 (tourist office)
🕐 Apr–Oct: 9–12 and 2–5; Nov–Mar: 2–4
🍴 Excellent cafés and restaurants in the area
🚉 Lier Station
♿ Few
✋ Moderate

St Gummaruskerk

Lier Town Hall with belfry

- ✉ Grote Markt 57
- ☎ 03–4883888 (tourist office)
- 🕐 Can be visited only with a town guide
- 🍴 Excellent cafés and restaurants in the area
- 🚉 Lier Station
- ♿ None
- 💰 Moderate

STADHUIS WITH BELFRY ✪✪
The imposing Town Hall with belfry attached dominates the Grote Markt at Lier. The Antwerp architect, Jan Pieter van Baurscheit, who built the Osterriethuis (► 58) in Antwerp, was awarded the contract to build the town hall in rococo style. The present building dates from 1740. The central section projects and is crowned with a triangular pediment with the town's coat of arms. The rose on the facade gives the height above sea level: 6m. The windows of the town hall consist of a total of 3,592 small panes. A notable feature of the interior is the rococo spiral staircase. It has only two points of support, one at the base and one at the top and it leads from the ground floor to the first floor. A painting on the ceiling in the council chamber illustrates the virtues and vices.

The Town Hall also has a hall used for weddings, with a life-size portrait of the writer Felix Timmermans painted by Baron Opsomer.

TIMMERMANS-OPSOMERHUIS ✪✪✪
The writer Felix Timmermans (1886–1947) and the painter Isodore Opsomer were good friends and regarded themselves as champions of Flemish cultural life. Timmermans wrote about traditional life in the Flemish countryside. His best-known work is *Pallieter*, which was banned by the Catholic Church when it appeared for being too frivolous. Opsomer is known for his portrayals of the sea and village life, though he also painted portraits, some of which are on display here. The ground floor has a sample of the work of the sculptor Lodewijk van Boeckel who was a friend of both men. Upstairs there is an overview of the work of Felix Timmermans together with first editions of his works.

A ticket for this museum also allows entrance to the Museum Wuyts (► 80).

- ✉ Netelaan 6
- ☎ 03–4911394
- 🕐 Apr–Oct: Tue–Thu and Sat–Sun 10–12 and 1–5:30; Nov–Mar: Sun 10–12 and 1:30–4:30
- 🍴 Excellent cafés and restaurants in the area
- 🚉 Lier Station
- ♿ Few
- 💰 Moderate

ZIMMERTOREN ✪✪✪

This is actually the Zimmertoren Corneliustoren, but is better known by its nickname. The tower is a remnant of the second town walls built in the 14th century. In 1930 Louis Zimmer gave the Jubelklok (Jubilee Clock) to commemorate a hundred years of the state of Belgium. The clock, which has 13 dials, was set in the facade of the Corneliustoren. You can of course read the hours, but there are also faces for the days of the week, the phases of the moon, the date, the tides in the River Nete and the signs of the zodiac. Figures appear out of the side of the tower depicting the life-cycle of man.

A side building houses the Wonderklok, another of Zimmer's timepieces dating from 1935; this one has 93 dials and 14 automata.

✉ Zimmerplein 18
☎ 03–4911395
🕐 Jan–Feb and Nov–Dec: 10–12 and 2–4; Mar–Oct: 10–12 and 2–5; Apr–Sep: 10–12 and 1–6
🍴 Excellent cafés and restaurants in the area
🚉 Lier Station
♿ Few
💶 Moderate

Zimmertoren with the Jubilee Clock

74A1

Hanswijkstraat

Always open, you can just wander round

Excellent cafés and restaurants in the area

All buses direction Grote Markt

Few

G. de Stassartstraat 153

015–290660

Sun–Thu 10–5, Fri 10–1

Excellent cafés and restaurants in the area

All buses direction Grote Markt

Few

Moderate

Mechelen

Mechelen (Malines) was once the capital of The Netherlands. Nowadays it is a pleasant provincial town with a wealth of historic buildings. It is less than 30km from Antwerp and is certainly worth visiting.

COMMANDERIE PITZEMBURG

This is the remains of the building complex of a German order of chivalry that existed during the time of the Crusades. One of the order's aims was to colonise Eastern Europe. The order founded an establishment at Mechelen on the Pitzenborgh. The noble members of the order had to take three oaths: obedience to their superiors, poverty, and celibacy. The last oath did not apply if the knight was the last male in his line. The chapel dates from 1451. In 1655 a square building in bluestone was erected at the entrance to the complex. You can walk from the Commanderie to the Stedelijke Kruidtuin (municipal herb garden, ➤ 88), which was formerly the garden of the Commanderie.

JOODS MUSEUM VAN DEPORTATIE EN VERZET

During the war there was a transit camp in the Dossinkazerne (Dossin Barracks) in Mechelen for the deportation of Belgian Jews. The museum gives a chronological summary of the *Endlösung*, the 'Final Solution' in Belgium and Europe. It begins with a presentation on the rich Jewish culture before

the war, how the German occupier, as in Germany, first deprived the Jews of their fundamental rights, turned the members of the Jewish community into pariahs and then tried to destroy them. The museum also recounts stories of heroism and sacrifice amidst the horror: resistance against the Nazis and how some Belgians, at the risk of their own lives, helped Jewish children.

Jewish Deportation and Resistance Museum

A Walk Through and Around Grote Markt in Mechelen

Start in Grote Markt (Market Place) in Mechelen and turn into Befferstraat, next to the Stadhuis.

St Romboutskathedraal (➤ 73, 86) is on the edge of the Grote Markt. It is the largest building in Mechelen and is visible from far outside the town. The Stadhuis (Town Hall) is also in the Grote Markt (➤ 87) as is the statue of the Margaret of Austria (➤ 89), governor of The Netherlands.

Befferstraat comes out into Veemarkt (Cattle Market) which has wonderful facades. Turn into Keizerstraat.

Befferstraat is one of the oldest streets in Mechelen. At the junction of Veemarkt with Blokstraat and Keizerstraat you will see the baroque St Pieter-en-Pauluskerk. The palaces of both Margaret of York and Margaret of Austria (➤ 89) stand in Keizerstraat.

Retrace your steps into Keizerstraat and go along Veemarkt in the direction of Biest. At the end cross diagonally to the right over Frederik de Merodestraat.

The Stadsmuseum Hof van Bus1eyden (➤ 88) just here is worth a visit. The white house on the corner of St Jansstraat is the Carillon School.

Turn left into St Jansstraat and then go right to Goswin de Stassartstraat.

Here you will find the Jewish Deportation and Resistance Museum (➤ 84), which you may want to visit.

After a visit to the Jewish Deportation and Resistance Museum retrace your steps into the Goswin de Stassartstraaat, walk back through St Jansstraat. Keep straight on to the Wolmarkt (Wool Market) which will bring you back to St Romboutskathedraal with the Grote Markt beyond it.

Distance
3–4km

Time
2–4 hours

Start/End point
Grote Markt
🚌 All buses direction Grote Markt

Lunch
De Beurs
✉ Grote Markt 10
☎ 015–203641

Statue of Margaret of Austria in Grote Markt, Mechelen

- ✉ Grote Markt
- ☎ 015–297655
- 🕐 10–12 and 1–5
- 🍴 Excellent cafés and restaurants in the area
- 🚌 All buses direction Grote Markt
- ♿ Good
- ✋ Moderate

ST ROMBOUTSKATHEDRAAL ★★★

The construction of the cathedral, in Brabant Gothic, lasted from the 13th to the 16th century. The cathedral was dedicated to St Rombout who converted the area to Christianity in the 8th century. The cathedral has a wonderful collection of works of art, including the painting *Christus aan het Kruis* (Christ on the Cross) by Antoon van Dyck. The choir aisle houses a collection of 25 panels with scenes from the life of St Rombout, which were painted by Colijn De Coter between 1480 and 1510.

St Romboutskathedraal in Mechelen dominates the skyline

The high altar was designed by Lucas Faydherbe, a pupil of Rubens. In addition there is a collection of silver from the 17th to 19th centuries and countless monuments to famous residents of Mechelen. At the back of the cathedral is a model of the tower which is 167m high. There is also an organ with 6,606 pipes. You can climb the cathedral tower but only if accompanied by a guide. During the climb the guide pauses six times in the various rooms in the tower to explain the skill of the crane builders. The tour guide leads you under the six chiming bells of the old carillon, past 43 other bells and the bell called Salvator, weighing 8,884kg and the old Jesus bell of 1460. Almost at the top of the tower you see the new carillon and can then enjoy a beautiful view of the town and beyond.

SPEELGOEDMUSEUM ✪✪✪

Children are of course mad about it but grown-ups too are very enthusiastic about the Toy Museum. It contains over 30 different sections spread over two floors, full of toys from today and long ago. It begins with the Pieter Brueghel painting *Traditionele Kinderspelen* (Traditional Children's Games), but it also has sections such as 'Mechanical and Tin Toys', 'Soldiers and Model Making', 'Dolls and Dolls' Houses', 'Soft Toys', 'Party Games and Puzzles' and so on. An attractive feature is that children are allowed to play with the toys which are not there just to look at. The museum also holds regular exhibitions organised on a particular theme.

- ✉ Nekkerspoelstraat 21
- ☎ 015–557075
- ⏰ Tue–Sun 10–5
- 🍴 Cafeteria (££) in the museum
- 🚉 Mechelen Nekkerspoel Station
- ♿ Good
- 💰 Moderate

STADHUIS ✪✪✪

The Town Hall is a closed complex in three parts. The first part, the right wing, was the Lakenhal (Cloth Hall), and dates back to 1311. In those days the tower served as a prison. Prisoners had to provide their own food. They used to let down a basket through the bars in the hope that someone below would put something in it. Mechelen wanted to have a big bell tower, like Bruges, but that did not happen because of lack of money.

The building of the second part began in the 16th century, and was intended as the palace of the Grote Raad (Great Council). The council never met there because less than 20 years later, in 1547, the work came to a halt. Construction began again in 1900, following the original plans. This long and drawn-out process means that, although the building forms a whole, the styles vary; the bell tower is Gothic with its baroque decoration which was added later; the palace that was completed at a later date is neo-Gothic. The third part of the Stadhuis was built as late as 1975. The interior is well worth a visit although it has to be with a guided tour.

- ✉ Grote Markt 21
- ☎ 015–297655 (tourist office)
- ⏰ Only by arrangement with the tourist office
- 🍴 Excellent cafés and restaurants in the area
- 🚌 All buses direction Grote Markt
- ♿ Good
- 💰 Moderate

The Town Hall in Mechelen contains a medley of building styles

✉ Fr. de Merodestraat 65
☎ 015–202004
🕐 Tue–Sun 10–6
🍴 Excellent cafés and
   restaurants in the area
🚌 All buses direction Grote
   Markt
♿ Few
💶 Moderate

STADSMUSEUM HOF VAN BUSLEYDEN ✪✪✪

The Hof van Busleyden was built at the beginning of the
16th century for Hieronymus Busleyden, a humanist and a
prominent member of the Great Council. Erasmus would
have stayed there several times. After Busleyden died the
building had various owners and uses until 1620 when it
was set up as Berg van Barmhartigheid. The Hof was badly
damaged during World War I. It was restored completely
in 1935 and since then it has been used as the town
museum. There is a model of Dijlestad (a former name for
Mechelen) circa 1800, with the wall intact. You can study
copies of the deeds and documents by which the town
was granted its freedom in the early Middle Ages. In a
historic section, light is shed on the heyday of Mechelen
during the reign of Margaret of Austria (1507–30) and there
is more detail about the importance of the Great Council,
the highest legal authority of the South Netherlands, on
which Busleyden had a seat.

✉ Bruul 129
🕐 8–sunset
   unrestricted access
🍴 Excellent cafés and
   restaurants in the area
🚉 Station Mechelen
   Centraal
♿ Few

STEDELIJKE KRUIDTUIN ✪✪✪

This used to be the garden belonging to the Commanderie
Pitzemburg (➤ 84). Old chronicles claim that the potato
'conquered' Europe from this garden in 1580. The herb
garden has an orangery, greenhouses and more than 200
different kinds of herbs. The inspiration for this garden
came from the plans of Rembertus Dodoens, a child
prodigy of the 16th century and author of the
Cruydenboek (*Herb Book*). Dodoens was scarcely 13
years old when he entered the University of Leuven
(Louvain) in 1530. He
published his first book,
also about herbs, three
years later. When he was
18 he qualified in medicine
at Leuven; he made a
number of journeys and
then returned in 1546
to his birthplace where
he became the town
physician. He was so
famous that the Emperor
Maximilian II took him to
Vienna as his personal
physician. At the end of
his life Dodoens was
a professor, teaching in
Leiden.

Mechelen herb garden

PALEIS VAN MARGARETHA VAN OOSTENRIJK

In 1507 Margaret of Austria moved to Mechelen as governor and from here she ruled The Netherlands in the name of her nephew Charles who was then a minor. Initially she lived in the Paleis van Magaretha van York (Margaret of York's Palace) in the same street. Straight away she had the architect Rombout Keldermans begin the construction of her own palace, which was later added to by the French architect Guyot de Beaugrant. So although most of the palace is in late Gothic style, the gate-house is one of the earliest Renaissance buildings in northern Europe. Emperor Charles V grew up in this palace. Since 1796 it has been used as a court of justice. It is not possible to visit the building without written permission from the chairman of the bench, which enables you to go into the lovely garden.

✉ Keizerstraat 20
☎ 015–288111
◷ Visits only with written permission from the chairman of the bench
🍴 Excellent cafés and restaurants in the area
🚌 All buses direction Grote Markt
♿ Few

Above: *the palace of Margaret of Austria*

TECHNOPOLIS

Technopolis is a hands-on centre for science and technology. The idea is that you can pick up and try out everything – there are 227 interactive exhibits in an area of 3,500sq m, and a house with all kinds of technical gadgets where you can even keep a television running by pedal power. There is information about solar energy, an aeroplane cockpit with a simulator, and a wealth of other stimulating exhibits.

Technopolis is wonderful for children but grown-ups think it is fantastic too. Each exhibit is designed so that children can reach it easily and yet adults never need to bend down.

✉ Technologielaan
☎ 015–342000
◷ 9:30–5. Closed 1 Jan, 25 and 31 Dec, Easter Day and the first week of September (Mon–Fri)
🍴 Cafeteria in the building
🚌 Bus 282, 283
♿ Good
💰 Moderate

Turnhout

Turnhout, 'the playing card town', probably already had settlers in the Bronze Age. We know for certain that between 1209 and 1213 Duke Henry I granted it the status of a town. It has never had walls and has suffered a great deal from raids and warfare. Today it is a pleasant provincial town with a popular pedestrianised shopping street.

➕ 74C2

✉ Druivenstraat 18
☎ 014–415621
🕐 Tue–Sun 2–5
🍴 Excellent cafés and restaurants in the area
♿ Few

NATIONAAL MUSEUM VAN DE SPEELKAART ⭐⭐⭐

This is a must for anyone visiting Turnhout. The basis for the graphics industry in the town was established by the printer Pieter Corbeels. Because of his part in the Boerenkring (▶ 77) the French beheaded Corbeels. His apprentice Phillippus Jacobus Brepols took over the business and made sure that the printing of playing cards in Turnhout grew into a proper industry.

In the National Playing Card Museum you will find an unbelievable collection of playing cards from Belgium as well as the rest of the world. You can watch videos that show how playing cards are made, and old printing presses will give you an idea of how it was done in the past. The museum is proud of its 18th-century steam engine that used to drive the old printing presses. Before you leave you can visit the museum shop and buy a pack of original Turnhout playing cards.

The Playing Card Museum in Turnhout with an original press for printing playing cards

---

✉ Patersstraat 100
☎ 014–443355
🕐 Office hours
🍴 Excellent cafés and restaurants in the area
♿ Few

PATERSPAND ⭐⭐

From 1899 to 1986, when the last monks left, the Paterspand (Fathers' House) was a house of the Friars Minor. It was later bought by the Association of Christian Employers who, after restoring it, set up their offices there. The dome of the courtyard garden is very striking. A metal construction links the buildings on either side. The present conference room was formerly a church. The garden has been replanned but the main elements have been kept.

Where To...

Above: in Antwerp you have a choice of so many
local beers that it would be impossible to sample
them all in one short visit

Right: a street musician adds to the atmosphere
on the Handschoenmarkt

Antwerp

Prices

With the exception of exclusive haute cuisine restaurants, eating out in Antwerp need not be expensive. What is more, you can expect excellent quality. You can eat very well for under 600 Belgium Francs per person. There is no need to tip although customers often round up the bill.

£ = up to 15 euros (BF600)

££ = between 15 euros (BF600) and 42 euros (BF1700)

£££ = above 42 euros (BF1700)

1200 ASA (£)

Trendy, southern bar serving food below the Museum voor Fotografie.

⊠ Waalse Kaai 44
☎ 03–2485902 🍴 Daily lunch and dinner. During winter closed Sun–Mon 🍷 4, 8

3 Fluwelen (£££)

Romantic restaurant with cosy library. Classic cuisine with a creative touch.

⊠ Hofstraat 24 ☎ 03–2340527
🍴 Tue–Fri lunch and dinner, Sat dinner 🍷 4, 7

Absoluut Zweeds (££)

Perfect Swedish cuisine. Enjoy a feast of fish in a minimalist setting.

⊠ Marnixplaats 14
☎ 03–2372843 🍴 Mon–Fri lunch and dinner, Sat dinner
🍷 4, 8

Allegria (££)

Artistic restaurant, the menu cover is a music score sheet and young musicians provide the atmosphere. You can admire or buy the paintings on the walls. Also excellent vegetarian cuisine.

⊠ Nassaustraat 15
☎ 03–2313158 🍴 Dinner
🍷 4, 7

Amadeus (££)

Old-fashioned reliability. Famous for *Ribbekens à volonté* (all-you-can-eat spare ribs).

⊠ St Paulusplaats 20
☎ 03–2322587 🍴 Dinner
🍷 4, 7

Amadeus (££)

Popular tearoom, ice-cream parlour and bar serving food. Speciality: jumbo mussels.

⊠ Jan Blomstraat 3–5
☎ 03–2340320 🍴 Tue–Sun 9:30AM–7PM 🍷 2, 11

Antoon van Dyck (£)

A tearoom, ice-cream parlour and restaurant in the painter's birthplace.

⊠ Grote Markt 4
☎ 03–2313565 🍴 Tue–Sun lunch and dinner 🍷 2, 11

Antwerps–Kaaps Degustatiehuis (££)

For homesick South Africans: springbok fillet and fresh fruit with an exquisite South African wine.

⊠ Breydelstraat 25
☎ 03–2313955 🍴 Wed–Mon lunch and dinner 🍷 2, 15

De Barbarie (£££)

An upmarket class restaurant with a beautiful garden. Speciality: Barbary duck.

⊠ Van Breestraat 4
☎ 03–2328198 🍴 Tue–Fri lunch and dinner, Sat dinner
🍷 7, 8

Bazilikum (££)

Bar serving food with the theme 'Fall of the Holy Roman Empire'. Complete with round table and burning torches on the walls.

⊠ Verschansingsstraat 61
☎ 03–2162869 🍴 Wed–Sun dinner 🍷 4, 8

The Bistro (££)

Near the Meir, the pedestrianised shopping street. A comprehensive menu and a lovely terrace for summer meals.

⊠ Wapper 1A
☎ 03–2323675
🍴 Daily breakfast, lunch and dinner 🍷 2, 15

Bistro Royal (££)

Popular restaurant with 'political-satirical' menu.

⊠ Veemarkt 27 ☎ 03–2328580
🍴 Wed–Mon lunch and dinner
🍷 4, 7

Bitterpeen (£££)
A popular restaurant with fine French cuisine, and if you are lucky, a jazz concert in the background.

IJzerlaan 26 ☎ 03–2274696 Mon–Fri lunch and dinner, Sat–Sun dinner 🚇 Antwerpen Dam Station

Bizzie Lizzie (£££)
Trendy brasserie in a vibrant neighbourhood with excellent Franco-Belgian cuisine.

Vlaamse Kaai 16 ☎ 03–2386197 Mon–Fri lunch and dinner, Sat dinner 🚋 4, 8

Den Blauwe Canard (£)
Specialities: duck, goose and foie gras. Light interior and a toaster on each table so you can make toast for the foie gras.

Ossenmarkt 28 ☎ 03–2324901 Mon–Sat lunch and dinner 🚋 4, 8

Botanica (££)
Classic cuisine in a romantic interior. In the summer you have a lovely view of the nearby Kruidtuin.

Leopoldstraat 24 ☎ 03–2251004 Daily lunch and dinner 🚋 7, 8

't Brantijser (££)
Bar with snacks and summery salads in 16th-century building in Antwerp's most attractive square.

Hendrik Conscienceplein 7 ☎ 03–2331833 Daily lunch and dinner 🚋 11

Brasserie Den Anversois (££)
A restaurant with a pleasant interior and a young team.

Specialities are omelettes and salads. There is always a bunch of flowers on the table.

Groenplaats 10 ☎ 03–2323371 Breakfast, lunch and dinner 🚋 2, 11, 15

Brasserie Marly (££)
Stylish restaurant for business lunches in an art deco interior.

Generaal Lemanlaan 64 ☎ 03–2812323 Mon–Fri lunch and dinner, Sat dinner 🚋 9

Brasserie van Loock (£££)
Young restaurant with a simple but very tasty cuisine. Specialities are fish dishes and sweetbreads.

Dageraadplaats 10–11 ☎ 03–2350158 Tue–Fri, Sun lunch and dinner, Sat dinner. Closed Mon 🚋 11

Brasseurs (££)
Near the law courts, so at lunchtime very popular with the legal fraternity of Antwerp.

Britselei 53 ☎ 03–2376901 Mon–Fri breakfast, lunch and dinner, Sun dinner 🚋 7, 8

Café Strauss (££)
Romantic restaurant-cum-coffee house with piano bar. The restaurant has an extensive game menu.

Grotesteenweg 565 ☎ 03–4499111 Daily lunch and dinner 🚋 9

Caribbean Inn (££)
Delicious Jamaican cuisine in a restored 16th-century chapel.

Korte Nieuwstraat 18–20–22 ☎ 03–2310377 Wed–Fri lunch and dinner, Sat and Mon dinner 🚋 2, 15

Eating Out With Children
Antwerp is an exceptionally child-friendly city. Most restaurants serve special children's menus. Sometimes the children get a toy, comic or a colouring book that they can take to the table.

Eating in the Street

Locals demand the same standards of a bag of chips as they do of a three-course menu in an expensive restaurant. Chips are fried twice to make them extra crisp. Ask for a bag of chips for the fun of it although they are easier to eat out of a box.

De Caveau (££)

Artistic favourite bar of the Flemish Opera with an extensive food and drink menu.

⌧ Van Ertbornstraat 2
☎ 03–2251609 🕔 Mon–Sat lunch and dinner. Closed holidays 🚊 11

La Ciboulette (£££)

Restaurant with southern atmosphere and neo-classical French cuisine. Also vegetarian dishes.

⌧ Plantin and Moretuslei 136
☎ 03–2700211
🕔 Mon–Fri lunch and dinner. Closed Sat–Sun 🚊 11

Comte Charbons (££)

Trendy bistro in a former coal warehouse, hence the name (*Comte Charbons* means 'Count Coal'). Plain honest dishes.

⌧ Vlaamse Kaai 6
☎ 03–2484715
🕔 Tue–Sun dinner. Closed Mon 🚊 4,8

Celtic Ireland (£)

Atmospheric Irish bar serving food, where you can enjoy Irish stew with Irish folk music in the background.

⌧ Groenplaats 1
☎ 03–2131450
🕔 Breakfast, lunch and dinner
🚊 2, 15

't Chouffe Café (£)

Very typical Belgian bar specialising in Walloon beers and cuisine with beer as an ingredient.

⌧ Grote Markt 29
☎ 03–2327973 🕔 Daily lunch and dinner 🚊 2, 15

Duizend en één £–££

Modern Arabic cuisine in a huge space with a ceiling like a desert tent.

⌧ Vlaamse Kaai 45A
☎ 03–2371001 🕔 Mon–Tue and Thu–Fri lunch and dinner, Sat–Sun dinner
🚊 4, 8

't Elfde Gebod (££)

Romantic brasserie behind a medieval facade, famous for the statues of saints ranged around the dining room.

⌧ Torfbrug 10 ☎ 03–2893466
🕔 Daily lunch and dinner
🚊 2, 11, 15

Fairfood (££)

A 'green' restaurant with a strongly vegetarian menu. Meat-eaters can enjoy lamb and chicken.

⌧ Graaf van Egmontstraat 60
☎ 03–2389296
🕔 Wed–Mon lunch and dinner
🚊 4, 8

Le Flageolet (£)

Trendy bar serving food with an upmarket sandwich bar downstairs.

⌧ Frankrijklei 29
☎ 03–2321412
🕔 Mon–Sat breakfast, lunch and dinner 🚊 11

De Foyer (££)

Stylish brasserie on the first floor of the Bourlaschouwburg.

⌧ Komedieplaats 18
☎ 03–2335517
🕔 Daily lunch and dinner
🚊 7, 8

Grand Café Leroy (££)

Artistically decorated grand café with international cuisine and a lovely terrace.

⌧ Kasteelpleinstraat 49
☎ 03–2261199
🕔 Daily lunch and dinner
🚊 7, 8

Grand Café Poesjkin (££)

Unexpected peace in a little 17th-century square behind an alleyway. At the weekend there is live music until the small hours.

✉ St Nicolaasplaats 3
☎ 03–2330673 🕓 Daily lunch and dinner 🚊 11

Greens (£££)

Exquisite brasserie catering for mainly business clientele, with large garden terrace. Specialities: fish and lobster.

✉ Mechelsesteenweg 76
☎ 03–2385151
🕓 Mon–Fri lunch and dinner, Sat dinner 🚊 7, 8

Haddock (££)

Local bar for people from the Law Courts. Many about to be sentenced have drunk their last glass in freedom here.

✉ Amerikalei 8
☎ 03–2377801 🕓 Mon–Fri lunch and dinner, Sat–Sun dinner 🚊 7, 8

Hangar 41 (££)

Grand café near the former Zuiderdokken, with international cuisine and a young professional clientele.

✉ St Michielskaai 41
☎ 03–2570918 🕓 Mon–Fri breakfast, lunch and dinner, Sat–Sun dinner 🚊 4

Harwich (£)

During the week this is a meeting place for business people in a hurry. At weekends Harwich becomes a disco.

✉ Ledeganckkaai 23
☎ 03–2381787 🕓 Daily lunch and dinner 🚊 4

Hoffy's Take Away (££)

A Jewish restaurant where they are happy to initiate tourists into the kosher traditions of Eastern Europe, Sephardic, Ashkenazic and Israeli dishes. Also takeaway.

✉ Lange Kievitstraat 52
☎ 03–2343535
🕓 Sun–Thu lunch and dinner, Fri lunch 🚊 2, 15

Hollywood Café (£)

Café with an American theme in the grounds of the Metropolis cinema complex. Modern American cuisine. Always open.

✉ Groenendaallaan 406
☎ 03–5416973 🕓 Daily breakfast, lunch and dinner
🚌 Bus near Metropolis

K. Zeppos (£)

Artistic bar serving food, named after a Flemish TV programme from the 1970s. In the evenings full of drama students from the nearby Studio Herman Teirlinck.

✉ Vleminckveld 78
☎ 03–2311789 🕓 Daily lunch and dinner 🚊 7, 8

De Kerselaar (£££)

Upmarket restaurant belonging to chef Yves Michiels. The expensive menu is more than worth the price. Before you order you are welcomed with a glass of excellent champagne.

✉ Grote Pieter Potstraat
☎ 03–2335969 🕓 Mon dinner, Tue–Fri lunch and dinner. Closed Sat–Sun 🚊 2

Kleine Bourla (£)

A trendy bistro in the shadow of the 'real' Bourlaschouwburg.

✉ Kelderstraat 3
☎ 03–2321632
🕓 Daily lunch and dinner
🚊 7, 8

Snacks in Cafés

Just as you can expect the chips you buy in the street to be of good quality, you can have a snack in most cafés even if they do not advertise food. This can range from homemade soup or a cheese dish to a portion of moussaka. Again the locals take food seriously and you can expect something delicious.

Vegetarian Food

Flemish cuisine is basically meat based, with rich sauces. However, vegetarians can come into their own in Antwerp. There are a number of excellent vegetarian restaurants and most others always have a couple of vegetarian dishes on the menu. If this is not the case it is perfectly in order to ask the chef for a vegetarian suggestion.

Kommilfoo (£££)

Upmarket restaurant, mainly for business people. There is a five-course menu for those with time to linger.

✉ **Vlaamse Kaai 17**
☎ **03–2373000** 🕐 **Tue–Sat lunch and dinner. Closed Sun–Mon** 🚊 **7, 8**

Milano (£££)

The best Italian cuisine. The restaurant is designed as an aristocrat's house. In the open kitchen you can see for yourself how the chef prepares your osso bucco.

✉ **Statiestraat 11**
☎ **03–2326743** 🕐 **Thu–Tue lunch and dinner** 🚊 **11**

Nick's Café (£)

During the day a busy bar serving food for businessmen, at night a trendy bar.

✉ **Waalse Kaai 18**
☎ **03–2483686** 🕐 **Mon–Fri lunch and dinner, Sat dinner** 🚊 **4, 8**

Noord (££)

Café-brasserie in an authentic Gothic building with a huge terrace. Large portions of Flemish cuisine.

✉ **Grote Markt 24**
☎ **03–2322816** 🕐 **Daily lunch and dinner** 🚊 **2, 11, 15**

Oi! Food&Booze (££)

Bizarre post-punk bistro in the heart of the red-light district. Nice open fire.

✉ **Kleine Kraaiwijk 10**
☎ **03–2310671** 🕐 **Apr–Oct: Wed–Mon lunch and dinner; Nov–Mar: Thu–Mon** 🚊 **4, 7**

Paeters Vaetje (£)

Bar in the shadow of the cathedral. Two kinds of homemade soup, plus salads and pastas.

✉ **Blauwmoezelstraat 1**
☎ **03–2318476** 🕐 **Daily lunch and dinner** 🚊 **2, 11, 15**

Paon Royal (££)

Near Antwerp Zoo. Classic cuisine, but known especially for its patisserie menu.

✉ **Koningin Astridplein 25**
☎ **03–2024581** 🕐 **Daily lunch and dinner** 🚊 **2, 15**

't Pakhuis (££)

Huge bar serving food with its own indoor brewery and all dishes served with the house beer.

✉ **Vlaamse Kaai 76**
☎ **03–2381240** 🕐 **Daily lunch and dinner** 🚊 **4, 8**

Patine (£)

Stylish wine bar with a lovely terrace, snacks, quiches and salads.

✉ **Leopold De Waelstraat 1**
☎ **03–2570919** 🕐 **Daily lunch and dinner** 🚊 **4, 8**

Pelgrom (£)

Bar-restaurant in medieval style in interconnected 15th-century cellars. Waiters are dressed in the style of Brueghel. Food strictly according to medieval recipes. Very popular with tourists.

✉ **Pelgrimstraat 15**
☎ **03–2340809** 🕐 **Daily lunch and dinner** 🚊 **2, 11, 15**

Rubens Inn (££)

Close by the Rubenshuis. A huge terrace with seating for 200 and an extensive Franco-Belgian menu.

✉ **Wapper 17**
☎ **03–2263327** 🕐 **Daily breakfast, lunch and dinner** 🚊 **2, 15**

WHERE TO EAT & DRINK

Spagettiworld (£)

Trendy pasta bar with a young clientele. You can eat late here.

✉ **Oude Koornmarkt 66**
☎ **03-2343801**
🕔 **Daily dinner**
🚊 **2, 11, 15**

Stadscafé Corsendonk (£–££)

Town café-bar with a lot of atmosphere, Corsendonk beer and a delicious menu.

✉ **Suikerrui 1** ☎ **03-2261391**
🕔 **Daily lunch and dinner**
🚊 **2, 11, 15**

Sushi Factory (£)

Super-clean minimalist restaurant with a takeaway. Cool bar where for 1 euro (BF45) a piece you can try ready-made sushi with a glass of Japanese beer.

✉ **Nationalestraat 54**
☎ **03-2130300** 🕔 **Daily lunch and dinner** 🚊 **2, 15**

Taki's Greek Kitchen (££)

Greek cuisine in a restaurant decorated with modern art. For lovers of lamb, meze, moussaka and souvlaki.

✉ **IJzeren Waag 1**
☎ **03-2133773** 🕔 **Daily lunch and dinner** 🚊 **4, 8**

Tam Lap Tai (££)

Pleasant Thai restaurant where the Thai community of Antwerp eats out at the weekend.

✉ **Van Wesebekestraat 13**
☎ **03-2319256**
🕔 **Daily lunch and dinner**
🚊 **2, 11**

Terra Meiga (£)

Atmospheric café with Celtic music in the background and a Spanish menu. *Terra Meiga* means both 'enchanted land' and 'Province of Galicia'.

✉ **Vlaamse Kaai 64**
☎ **03-2487371**
🕔 **Wed–Fri lunch and dinner, Sat–Sun dinner**
🚊 **4, 8**

Ultimatum (££)

Trendy, centrally situated bistro on the Grote Markt with a view of the Stadhuis, Hoogstraat, Suikerrui and the Scheldekaaien.

✉ **Grote Markt 8**
☎ **03-2325853**
🕔 **Sun–Fri lunch and dinner, Sat breakfast, lunch and dinner**
🚊 **2, 11, 15**

Wok en 't Tafeldier (££)

Asian kitchen where you can choose the ingredients for your own dish and then watch the chef prepare it.

✉ **Gentplaats 1**
☎ **03-2489595**
🕔 **Sat–Thu dinner, Fri lunch and dinner**
🚊 **4, 8**

Wok-A-Way (£)

Asian fast-food restaurant with a rolling counter, flickering TV screens and delicious wok dishes.

✉ **Groendalstraat 14**
☎ **03-2131313**
🕔 **Mon–Sat lunch and dinner**
🚊 **2**

Zuiderterras (££)

Built in the shape of a ship by the architect van Reeth. Classical to modern menu and a wonderful view over the Scheldt.

✉ **Ernest van Dijckkaai 37**
☎ **03-2341275**
🕔 **Daily breakfast, lunch and dinner** 🚊 **4**

International Dishes

As a seaport Antwerp has always had an international character. This is reflected in the great variety of ethnic restaurants: Chinese, Japanese, Moroccan, Lebanese, Persian, Thai, Greek, Swedish… Antwerp has them all.

Restaurants outside Antwerp

Opening Times

In most Flemish towns, not just in Antwerp, you can always get a meal somewhere whatever the time. Breakfast bars and bars serving food mostly open from 7AM and serve substantial omelettes, lunch begins at 11:30AM and usually lasts until 2:30PM. You can have dinner from 5:30PM until late into the night.

Geel

Arco Baleno (££)

Atmospheric Italian restaurant with an art deco interior. The house speciality is ravioli with wild mushrooms.

✉ Pas 123 ☎ 014–582555
🕔 Sun–Mon and Wed–Fri lunch and dinner, Sat dinner

Brasserie Flore (££)

Busy brasserie in the market place, with a terrace.

✉ Markt 52 ☎ 014–588080
🕔 Daily breakfast, lunch and dinner

China (££)

Excellent Chinese restaurant with more than 100 dishes on the menu. Specialities include dim sum, filled crab claws and glazed duck.

✉ Nieuwstraat 38
☎ 014–580209 🕔 Mon–Tue and Thu–Sun lunch and dinner

De Cuylhoeve (£££)

Rustic romantic upmarket restaurant in the woods of Geel. Has an outstanding menu and perfect service. On warm days you can eat in the garden.

✉ Hollandsebaan 7
☎ 014–585735 🕔 Mon–Tue and Thu–Fri lunch and dinner, Sat dinner

De Malle Kok (£££)

Inventive Franco-Belgian dishes in novel interior with open kitchen. Friendly atmosphere and a pleasant terrace.

✉ Peperstraat 27 ☎ 014–586324 🕔 Tue–Sun lunch and dinner

Hoogstraten

De Tram (££)

Classic Franco-Belgian cuisine in a traditional establishment.

De Tram has been open for 75 years and also has five rooms to let (➤ 102).

✉ Vrijheid 192 ☎ 03–3146565
🕔 Wed–Sun lunch and dinner

Lier

De Broodtafel (£)

Classic vegetarian cuisine with seasonal specialities. De Broodtafel is also an excellent place for breakfast.

✉ Vismarkt 29 ☎ 03–4885026
🕔 Mon and Wed–Sat breakfast, lunch and dinner, Sun breakfast

't Cleyn Paradijs (£££)

Unusual restaurant at the foot of the St Gummaruskerk. A lot of atmosphere. Menu is classic-modern and good value.

✉ Heilige Geeststraat 2
☎ 03–4807857 🕔 Thu–Mon lunch and dinner

Land van Belofte (£££)

French cuisine with a preference for Provençal dishes. The menu changes each month.

✉ Begijnhofstraat 7
☎ 03–4882256 🕔 Wed–Fri and Sun lunch and dinner, Sat dinner

Numerus Clausus (££)

Friendly family bistro in a plain setting.

✉ Keldermansstraat 2 ☎ 03–4802182 🕔 Tue–Sat lunch

Plantage (££)

First floor restaurant with an open kitchen and British colonial decor. Classic-modern dishes.

✉ Grote Markt ☎ 03–4881900
🕔 Wed–Fri lunch and dinner, Sat dinner

De Werf (£££)

Pleasant restaurant with a view of the Zimmertoren.

✉ **Werf 17** ☎ **03–4807190**
🕐 **Sun–Tue and Fri lunch and dinner, Sat dinner**

Zuid–West (£££)

Luxurious brasserie run by the owner of mega discotheque La Rocca. Zuid-West consists of several interconnecting rooms each with its own decor. Cuisine is very visually appealling.
✉ **Antwerpsesteenweg 330**
☎ **03–4891300** 🕐 **Daily lunch and dinner**

Mechelen
Camogli (££)

Friendly restaurant with a terrace. Italian cuisine with a choice of 15 kinds of pasta.
✉ **Leopoldstraat 48** ☎ **015–430730** 🕐 **Daily lunch and dinner**

De Cirque (££)

Bar serving food with tacos as a speciality. Jazz on the first Sunday of each month.
✉ **Vismarkt 8** ☎ **015–207780**
🕐 **Daily lunch and dinner**

De Graspoort (££)

Alternative restaurant with vegetarian dishes. The owners are especially proud of their filled pancakes.
✉ **Leopoldstraat 48** ☎ **015–430730** 🕐 **Daily lunch and dinner**

D'Hoogh (£££)

Luxury high class restaurant run by the chef Erik D'Hoogh in an imposing listed building from the beginning of the 20th century. The dining room is on the first floor.
✉ **Grote Markt 19** ☎ **015–217553** 🕐 **Tue–Fri lunch and dinner, Sat dinner, Sun lunch**

Egmond and Hoorne (££)

Reliable restaurant with Flemish cuisine: chips and mussels, steak and fish.

Homemade ice cream served for desert.
✉ **Befferstraat 20** ☎ **015–216127** 🕐 **Daily lunch and dinner**

Gulden Rabat (££)

Reliable fish restaurant with an art deco interior. Try the mussels in season.
✉ **Vismarkt 16** ☎ **015–204635**
🕐 **Wed–Fri and Sun lunch and dinner, Sat dinner**

Ludovic (£££)

Franco-Belgian cuisine in a castle on the outskirts of Mechelen. It has a park and a modern orangery.
✉ **Antwerpsesteenweg 92**
☎ **015–209582** 🕐 **Tue–Sun lunch and dinner**

De Maretak (£££)

Classic Franco-Belgian restaurant opposite the archbishop's palace. A light and spacious dining room with round tables. The service can be slow but the food is excellent.
✉ **Wollenmarkt 22–24** ☎ **015–276662** 🕐 **Daily lunch and dinner**

Turnhout
D'Achterkeuken (££)

Romantic restaurant with style. Specialities: salad with calves' sweetbreads, veal steaks with scampi in pepper sauce and fish in lemon butter sauce.
✉ **Baron du Fourstraat 4**
☎ **014–438642** 🕐 **Wed–Mon lunch and dinner**

Boeket (£££)

Modern restaurant with garden in a villa north of Turnhout. Perfect service and a chef who takes his job extremely seriously.
✉ **Klein Engeland 67** ☎ **014–427028** 🕐 **Fri and Sun–Tue lunch and dinner, Thu and Sat dinner**

Credit Cards (▶ 101)

Most restaurants will accept credit cards but most bars serving food do not. Restaurants that take cards display clearly the logos of the ones they will accept. If you want to pay by credit card it is better to ask if you may before you order. Many restaurants will not take credit cards for less than BF1,000 even if you can see the logo of your credit card company on the door.

Antwerp

Prices

The prices of hotels include VAT and breakfast is usually included but it is better to check beforehand. The following categories are for a room:

£ = up to 50 euros (BF2,000)

££ = between 50 euros (BF2,000) and 124 euros (BF5,000)

£££ = more than 124 euros (BF5,000)

Astrid Park Plaza Hotel (£££)

A luxury 229-room hotel in the style of the big hotels in the US. This was designed by the celebrated American architect Michael Graves. The restaurant has a fantastic view over Centraal Station.

✉ **Koningin Astridplein 7**
☎ 03–2031234 📺 2, 11

Colombus (££)

Pleasant business hotel with 32 rooms, cable TV, friendly staff and a swimming pool.

✉ **Frankrijklei 4**
☎ 03–2330390 📺 2, 11

Hilton Antwerp (£££)

A top hotel in the Grand Bazaar building, close to the cathedral. For the luxury hotel experience. Ask for special weekend rates.

✉ **Groenplaats** ☎ 03–2041200
📺 2, 15

Hotel Rubens (£££)

Romantic hotel in the heart of Antwerp. You are given a glass of sherry when you check in. Breakfast is served on the patio under the 16th-century tower. The rooms could be larger.

✉ **Oude Beurs 29**
☎ 03–2224848 📺 2, 11, 15

Hotel Tulip Inn Antwerp Docklands (££)

Modern business hotel with Philippe Starck furniture and office facilities in the rooms. Reasonable prices but it is quite a way to walk to the centre of the city.

✉ **Kempisch Dok Westkaai 84–90** ☎ 03–2310726 📺 4, 7

Ibis (££)

Sound, slightly impersonal business hotel, within walking distance of the Meir, by the theatre square.

✉ **Meistraat 39**
☎ 03–2318830 📺 2, 15

Prinse (££)

Romantic and rustic at the same time. Prinse is in the heart of the student quarter but once inside the 16th-century building the city seems miles away.

✉ **Keizerstraat 63**
☎ 03–2264050 📺 4

Radisson SAS Park Lane Hotel (£££)

Luxury business hotel with a view of the Stadspark. Rooms and service are immaculate but you pay for it.

✉ **Van Eycklei 34**
☎ 03–2858585 📺 2, 15

't Sandt (£££)

Romantic luxury with historic decor. The hotel has a beautiful garden.

✉ **Zand 17–19** ☎ 03–2329390
📺 4

Scheldezicht (££)

Very pleasant family hotel close by Vrijdagmarkt and Grote Markt. All the rooms have an en suite shower, washbasin and sitting area.

✉ **St Jansvliet 12**
☎ 03–2316602 📺 2, 11, 15

Stijlvolle Gastenkamers (£££)

Be a paying guest in a stately country house dating from 1889. There are two beautiful rooms with TV and jacuzzi, but only two, so reservations recommended.

✉ **Amerikalei 103**
☎ 03–2161480
📺 7, 8

Ter Elst (££)

A lovely hotel, in a rural setting with spacious rooms and reasonable prices but to visit the centre of Antwerp you will need to take a taxi.

✉ **Terelststraat 310, 2650 Edegem** ☎ **03–4509000** 🛏 **32**

Witte Lelie (£££)

One of the most fashionable and most romantic hotels in Antwerp in a beautifully restored 16th-century building. For dinners in evening dress and a brandy by the open fire.

✉ **Keizerstraat 16–18** ☎ **03–2261966** 🛏 **4**

B&B and Hostels
Bed & Breakfast (£)

Two guest rooms in an artist's house with a beautiful inner courtyard. Situated in the heart of trendy Antwerp South district. Book in advance.

✉ **Verschansingsstraat 55** ☎ **03–2480913** 🛏 **4, 8**

Boomerang (£)

Old fashioned, ridiculously cheap youth hostel with a 1960s atmosphere. 60 beds in five rooms. One of the rooms is reserved for women only.

✉ **Volkstraat 49** ☎ **03–2384782** 🛏 **4, 8**

Camping De Molen (£)

On the St Annastrand, on the left bank, with a lovely view of the quays of Antwerp on the other side of the Scheldt. The city is only a tram ride away.

✉ **St Annastrand, Jachthavenweg 2** ☎ **03–2198179** 🚋 **2, 3, 15**

Camping Vogelzang (£)

Just outside the Ring Road, but still between the busy main roads. If you dislike the noise of traffic at night, use earplugs. In the early morning you can count on birdsong as the Nachtegalen-park is nearby.

✉ **Vogelzanglaan** ☎ **03–2385717** 🚋 **2**

Jeugdherberg Opsinjoorke (£)

Youth hostel with dormitories for 13 and four double rooms. Basically closes at midnight and entrance is then by code number.

✉ **Eric Sasselaan 2** ☎ **03–2380273** 🛏 **8** 🚉 **Antwerpen-Zuid Station**

New International Youth Hotel (£)

For the backpacker who wants a little more comfort than is found in the normal youth hostel. Clean rooms with telephone and a communal TV lounge.

✉ **Provinciestraat 256** ☎ **03–2300522** 🛏 **11**

Rubenshof (£)

A real must! Rubens never came here, but the 19th-century dwelling house exudes a romantic atmosphere and the rooms are lovely at a reasonable price.

✉ **Amerikalei 115–117** ☎ **03–2370789** 🛏 **7, 8**

Zeemanshuis (£)

You won't meet many seamen here but plenty of tourists. Central situation with reasonable prices.

✉ **Falconrui 21** ☎ **03–2342603** 🛏 **7**

Credit Cards

Most hotels accept credit cards. If you want to book by phone many hotels prefer credit cards to cash. On arrival an imprint is taken of your credit card and you sign for the whole amount on departure. Clients who want to pay in cash or with travellers cheques may be asked to pay in advance.

Outside Antwerp

Booking Through a Tourist Office

It is not always easy to book a room in high season. For a small commission the local tourist office can help. The numbers are given below:

Tourist offices
Antwerp: 03-2320103
Geel: 014-570950
Herentals: 014-219088
Lier: 03-4883888
Mechelen: 015-297655

Hoogstraten
De Tram (££)
Pension with clean rooms, showers en suite and breakfast.
- ✉ Vrijheid 192
- ☎ 03–3146565

Geel
Hotel Claridge (££)
Business hotel with some tourists at the weekend. Price includes breakfast, all rooms have TV and telephone. Hotel Claridge is 3km from the centre of Geel.
- ✉ Antwerpseweg 101
- ☎ 014–582111

Herentals
Aldhem Hotel (£££)
Leisure hotel 15 minutes from Antwerp for a cycling and walking holiday in the woods of Kempen. Luxurious rooms and an upmarket restaurant.
- ✉ Jagersdreef 1, 2280 Grobbendonk ☎ 014–501001

Camping De Brink (£)
Modern camping complex 3km from Herentals. Seven camping areas, main building for up to a hundred people on full board, a log cabin and you can also rent an apartment in the week.
- ✉ VVKSM Jeugdverblijfcentrum De Brink, Bosbergen 1
- ☎ 014–211533

De Swaen I (£££)
Business hotel with few tourists. Luxurious rooms with bath, TV, telephone with outside line, minibar and safe.
- ✉ Belgiëlaan 1
- ☎ 014–225639

De Swaen II (££)
The same rooms as in De Swaen I, but cheaper because there is no lift in this hotel.
- ✉ Belgiëlei 3 ☎ 014–225639

De Zalm (££)
New hotel in the heart of the town, right on the Grote Markt.
- ✉ Grote Markt 21
- ☎ 014–286000

Lier
Handelshof (££)
Pleasant small hotel right opposite the station in Lier. The rooms were renovated recently and all have shower and/or bath.
- ✉ Leopoldplein 39–41
- ☎ 03–4800310

Hof van Aragon (££)
Sixteen-room hotel close to the Grote Markt. A business hotel during the week with mainly tourists at weekends.
- ✉ Mofdijk 4
- ☎ 03–4910800

Mechelen
Fran van Buggenhout, furnished studios (££)
Furnished studios with a well-filled fridge for breakfast. Suitable for families of up to five people.
- ✉ Straatje zonder einde 3
- ☎ 0476–264592

Golden Tulip Alfa Alba Hotel (££)
Efficient hotel with 43 rooms. Double rooms have shower and bath, single rooms have bath only. TV in all rooms. Dogs allowed.
- ✉ Korenmarkt 22–24
- ☎ 015–420303

Gulden Anker Best Western Hotel (££)
Hotel and restaurant with

traditionally-furnished rooms, but service is hurried.

✉ **Ridder Dessainlaan 2**
☎ **015–422535**

Hotel Carolus (££)

Sound hotel, just outside the town centre but still 'within the walls' of Mechelen. All rooms have TV and shower.

✉ **Guido Gezellelaan 49**
☎ **015–203880**

Hotel Domein Montreal (£££)

Hotel outside the centre of Mechelen. A little expensive for what is on offer, especially if the situation is taken into account. Staff are not always very friendly.

✉ **Duivenstraat 56**
☎ **015–204077**

Hotel Egmont (££)

Business hotel with weekend reductions. Good value for money. Price includes breakfast. TV in all rooms.

✉ **Oude Brusselstraat 50**
☎ **015–421399**

Hotel Hobbit (££)

Business hotel 3km from the town centre. All rooms have TV and telephone, and bathroom with bath and shower.

✉ **Battelsesteenweg 455 F**
☎ **015–272027**

Hotel In Den Bonten Os (££)

Business hotel 10km from Mechelen. Special rates apply at weekends. All rooms are fully equipped with TV, telephone, video, bathroom with shower and bath and a separate toilet.

✉ **Rijmenamseweg 214, 2820 Bonheiden**
☎ **015–520450**

Hotel Muske Pitter (££)

Small family hotel with four rooms. Very nice but usually fully booked.

✉ **Hanswijkstraat 70**
☎ **015–436303**

Op-Sinjoor (££)

Bed and breakfast in three rooms let by the Swinnen-Gijbels family of Mechelen. Price includes breakfast.

✉ **Leegheid 21**
☎ **0486–513346**

Refugie Lindenhof (££)

Bed and breakfast in three rooms for a maximum of six people in an annexe in the garden of the Vermeulen family. Centre of Mechelen 3km away.

✉ **Marterstraat 1**
☎ **015–271477**

Turnhout

Ter Driezen (££)

Plain business hotel with reasonable service, a restaurant, breakfast. Dogs are allowed.

✉ **Herentalsstraat 18**
☎ **014–420357**

Terminus (££)

Right on the Grote Markt, with facilities for people with disabilities. Dogs are allowed.

✉ **Grote Markt 72**
☎ **014–412078**

Viane (££)

Business hotel with good facilities for people with disabilities, and an indoor swimming pool.

✉ **Korte Vianestraat 2**
☎ **014–414748**

Guest Rooms

Apart from hotels, Flanders also provides the opportunity to stay in a guest room in a private house. This gives a unique insight into Flemish life. Enquire from the tourist office about guest rooms near your destination.

Art, Bygones & Antiques

Antiques

Antwerp is a wonderful place for antiques. In Kloosterstraat (➤ 50) you will find one shop after another to browse in. Enthusiasts can spend days here and still not see everything.

Blue Classics Antiques

British antiques: Chesterfields, Lloyd Loom wickerwork chairs, wooden cupboards.

✉ **Kloosterstraat 12**
☎ **03–2310836** 🚊 **4, 8**

Brocanteur Superieur

A shop for browsing where you might come across anything from a pipe-rack or plant stand to a counter devoted to stuffed birds.

✉ **Kloosterstraat 64–65**
☎ **03–2486987** 🚊 **4, 8**

Delphic Antiques

An antique shop selling some furniture but actually specialising in collector's items such as rare prints and watercolours.

✉ **Kloosterstraat 60**
☎ **03–2488749** 🚊 **4, 8**

Dock's for Antiques

Larger items of antique furniture for those who still have room for them. Shipping can sometimes also be arranged.

✉ **Kloosterstraat 13**
☎ **03–2332669** 🚊 **4, 8**

Cheffertons

A lovely shop that looks more like an exhibition gallery than an antique shop, with mahogany furniture from the 18th and 19th centuries, antique silver, old chandeliers and candle sticks.

✉ **Groendalstraat 16**
☎ **03–2326920** 🚊 **2, 15**

Hamptons

No displays full to bursting here, the owner has set it out as if this was a room in his own house.

✉ **Kloosterstraat 13**
☎ **0476–240689** 🚊 **4, 8**

Hot & Cold, New & Old

Antique ornamental items, especially for the bathroom.

✉ **Kloosterstraat 66**
☎ **03–2570031** 🚊 **4, 8**

M: Bascourt

English and continental European 17th- and 18th-century antiques, Delft pottery and Chinese porcelain. The shop looks more like a museum than an antique shop and if you ask the owner for information you will get a wealth of advice.

✉ **Mechelsesteenweg 17**
☎ **03–2337120** 🚊 **7, 8**

Moby Dick

Antwerp wouldn't be a world-class seaport without a marine antique shop. You can find ships in bottles, brass sextants, old compasses and much more.

✉ **St Jorispoort 13**
☎ **03–2271157** 🚊 **7, 8**

Oude Borze

Shop specialising in books, maps and old prints with the emphasis on items from Antwerp itself.

✉ **Oude Beurs 62**
☎ **03–2319474** 🚊 **2, 11, 15**

Oude Bureau's

A paradise for writers of travel guides! Beautiful writing tables, filing cabinets and reading lamps for the study.

✉ **Kloosterstraat 68–79**
☎ **0476–335932** 🚊 **4, 8**

Serafijn

Shop to browse in for antique glass and place settings.

✉ **Museumstraat 8**
☎ **03–2571048** 🚊 **4, 8**

Oude Spiegels
The name says it all: antique mirrors (*spiegels*), mirrors and more mirrors.

- ✉ **Kloosterstraat 68–79**
- ☎ **0476–335932**
- 🚊 **4, 8**

Tony Bogaert
Shop to browse round with a bit of everything: antiques, bygones, exotic items. For fanatical browsers.

- ✉ **Kloosterstraat 81**
- ☎ **03–2378955**
- 🚊 **4, 8**

Afric Art
Authentic West African objects, as they say 'no tourist junk' but genuine crafts.

- ✉ **Pourbusstraat 8**
- ☎ **03–2263377** 🚊 **4, 8**

Casbah
Moroccan furniture and ornaments at reasonable prices.

- ✉ **Kloosterstraat 52**
- ☎ **075–356838** 🚊 **4, 8**

Casa Maya
Gift shop with pots, vases, statues and masks, mainly from the Maya, Aztec and Inca traditions.

- ✉ **Melkmarkt 21**
- ☎ **03–2271755** 🚊 **11**

Fiftie–Fiftie
Kitsch from the 1950s, from Marilyn Monroe knick-knacks including a red-lipped sofa. It is worth seeing just for the window display. For anyone who wants to relive rock and roll.

- ✉ **Kloosterstraat 187**
- 🚊 **4, 8**

Maseda Trading
Art and utensils from southern Africa at reasonable prices. Everything from carving from Zimbabwe to masks from Gabon.

- ✉ **Steenhouwervest 30**
- ☎ **03–2272444**
- 🚊 **4, 8**

Mixtli
Not everything dates from the time of the Aztecs but the stock is imported directly from Mexico.

- ✉ **Reyndersstraat 8**
- ☎ **03–2132940**
- 🚊 **2, 11, 15**

Nour Assahrae
All kinds of Moroccan items. The cellar is set out like a genuine Moroccan salon.

- ✉ **Steegsken 7**
- ☎ **03–2261174** 🚊 **4, 8**

Rolies Ancient Art
You don't need to buy, fortunately. The owners are happy to talk about an Egyptian sarcophagus at 74,370 euros (BF3 million) or a Roman satyr at 13,875 euros (BF600,000). This is really a mini museum.

- ✉ **Wijngaardstraat 16–18**
- ☎ **03–2315162** 🚊 **11**

Steen and Been
A shop for fossils and shells including a mammoth bone and a set of shark's teeth.

- ✉ **Volkstraat 59**
- ☎ **03–2372522**
- 🚊 **4, 8**

Witte Uil
The place to go for cheap ethnic clothing and objects. It used to be a mecca for hippies; now attracts a wider public.

- ✉ **Kammenstraat 14–16**
- ☎ **03–2332436**
- 🚊 **2, 15**

Ethnic Antwerp
Antwerp, with its international character, is pre-eminently the place for ethnic art and items. Whatever you are looking for: a Japanese rice mat, an African fetish, a Mexican amulet or a Moroccan carpet, you will find it in Antwerp.

Clothes, Jewellery & Accessories

The 'Antwerp Six'
Bikkembergs, Demeulemeester, van Bierendonck, van Noten, van Saene and Yee are the six designers who have put Antwerp on the fashion map. In 1988 these six graduates from the City Fashion Academy had a stand together at Fashion Week in London. The British fashion journalists had a problem with the Flemish names, so the group was dubbed 'The Antwerp Six'.

Ann Demeulemeester
A 600sq m showroom displaying everything the Antwerp fashion industry has to offer: collections for women and men, but also shoes and accessories; designer tables too.

✉ **Hoek Leopold De Waelplaats-Verlatstraat**
☎ **03–2160133**
🖥 **4, 8**

Anvers
The designers Ann Kegels and Martine Hillen show their clothing lines in a former art gallery. They are also happy to provide information on their forthcoming collection.

✉ **Leopoldstraat 53**
☎ **03–2132808** 🖥 **4, 8**

Babes Store
Girls' shop for the 'girl-power' generation. The latest trends and accessories.

✉ **Kammenstraat 32**
☎ **03–2260231**
🖥 **2, 15**

Coccodrillo
The first shop in Antwerp for fashion shoes by top designers. According to the owners, Japanese tourists come to Antwerp specially to buy shoes in this shop.

✉ **Schuttershofstraat 9A**
☎ **03–2332093** 🖥 **2, 15**

Darcis
Top address for women with classic, stylish but expensive tastes. Darcis for men is opposite.

✉ **Frankrijklei 35–37**
☎ **03–2263458** 🖥 **2, 11, 15**

Erotische verbeelding
Stylishly decorated business selling erotica run by two ladies: the usual toys and a collection of sexy lingerie, including more ample sizes.

✉ **IJzerenwaag 10–12**
☎ **03–2268950** 🖥 **2, 15**

Extreme
Trendy skate/inline/BMX shop for shoes, trousers, boards, skid-lids, rucksacks, wheels, videotapes, knee protectors and much more.

✉ **Kammenstraat 46**
☎ **03–2332306** 🖥 **2, 15**

Fish&Chips
Called a supermarket for lifestyles in the new millennium. Sales of trendy clothing, a hairdresser, an underground art gallery and a DJ who contributes to the atmosphere.

✉ **Kammenstraat 26–38**
☎ **03–2270824** 🖥 **2, 15**

Jewel in a Box
Second-hand jewellery shop. Locals who want to sell jewellery can rent one of the little display boxes in the window.

✉ **Schuttershofstraat 34A**
☎ **03–2895610** 🖥 **2, 15**

Kousencenter
Socks, tights and underwear fill the entire shop. The manageress is happy to help anyone who gets lost amongst the racks.

✉ **Korte Gasthuisstraat 33**
☎ **03–2011670** 🖥 **2, 15**

Kwesto
Prestigious Italian women's fashion and a limited range of in-house designs. Nice but not cheap.

✉ **Huidevetterstraat 45**
☎ **03–2334676**
🖥 **2, 15**

Louis
The place to be for a sample of what the Belgian fashion industry has to offer, from Ann Demeulemeester to A.F. Vandervorst, if you don't want to trek round each of the designer shops.
✉ **Lombardenstraat 2**
☎ **03–2329872** 🚃 **2, 15**

Modepaleis
Home of Dries van Noten who also designs wonderful window displays.
✉ **Nationalestraat 16**
☎ **03–2339437** 🚃 **2, 15**

Naughty I
Alternative clothing at reasonable prices. The shop assistant also chooses the music.
✉ **Kammenstraat 67**
☎ **03–2133590**
🚃 **2, 15**

Optiek Somers
Showcase for well-known locals such as Boogie Boy, Tom Lanoye, Eric Melaerts, Joyce Smeets and Geert Hoste.
✉ **Eiermarkt 33** ☎
03–2334758
🚃 **2, 15**

Oxford
For the better British men's clothing, including made-to-measure in two weeks.
✉ **Huidevetterstraat 55**
☎ **03–2339097**
🚃 **2, 15**

Percy's
Shoe shop for men, with all the good makes.
✉ **Mechelsesteenweg 97**
☎ **03–2340017**
🚃 **7, 8**

Pomellato
Trendy designer jewellery in heavy gold. Pomellato also has a fun young collection but none of the stock is cheap.
✉ **Leopoldstraat 1**
☎ **03–2131790** 🚃 **7, 8**

Slaets Horlogerie
This jewellers is more than 50 years old, has its own workshop for clocks and watches and sells exclusive makes such as Blancpain, Cartier and Gucci.
✉ **De Keyzerlei 42**
☎ **03–2135081** 🚃 **2, 15**

The Factory
Trendy clothing shop for young people. Sole importer of the London label Hysteric Glamour in Antwerp.
✉ **Nationalestraat 76–78**
☎ **03–2132803**
🚃 **2, 15**

Verso
Designer shop which stocks all the top men's couturiers. This fashion is not cheap but Verso has nothing against you looking around. However if you take half the stock to the fitting room it is expected that you will buy something afterwards.
✉ **Huidevettersstraat 39**
☎ **03–2269292** 🚃 **2, 15**

Walter
Home base for the futuristic king of fashion Walter van Bierendonck. Here you will find what other trendy clothing shops will have on their rails in Kammenstraat next year.
✉ **St Antoniusstraat 12**
☎ **03–2132644** 🚃 **2, 15**

The Wilde Zee
The name of the quarter with the narrow pedestrian streets behind Huidevetter-straaat, Meirbrug and Schoenmarkt. This is a mecca for fashion junkies in Antwerp. All the collections are here, of course including the Antwerp Six, but also new, young talent.

Food & Drink

Chocolate
Belgian chocolate is renowned all over the world.
Belgians eat 7.8kg per head annually, so it is hardly surprising consumption on that scale has given rise to a high-level trade. On the Meir you can buy a box of pralines made by one of the great names in Belgian chocolate. You can also go in search of the genuine handmade product.

Andes Pacifico
The best of Latin America, imported direct. From Chilean *Tarapaca* and *Valvidieso* to *Yerba Maté*, a stimulating gaucho tea that purifies the blood.
✉ Provinciestraat 11
☎ 03–2363033
🚋 4, 8

Bakkerij Goossens
Real Antwerp bakers for rye bread, croissants and coffee cakes made with butter.
✉ Korte Gasthuisstraat 31
☎ 03–2260791
🚋 2, 15

La Bonbonnière
Old-fashioned sweet shop selling confectionary with a nostalgic flavour.
✉ Korte Gasthuisstraat 41
☎ 03–2331308
🚋 2, 15

Chacalli
Wine shop calling itself a vinothèque; you can taste a wide range of wines at the huge wooden tables. There are bowls discreetly provided should you wish to spit out the sample.
✉ Generaal Belliardstraat 9
☎ 03–2034950
🚋 7, 4

De Cognatheek
More than 100 brandies and 50 varieties of Pineau de Charente.
✉ Steenhouwervest 27
☎ 03–2328890
🚋 4, 8

Goossens Chocolatier
Belgian chocolate from a master confectioner.
✉ Issabellalei 61
☎ 03–2391310 🚋 2

Kaaps Wynhuys
Since the boycott of South African produce was lifted we have been able once again to enjoy these fine wines. Tasting sessions are organised here on the first Saturday of each month.
✉ Lange Nieuwstraat 31/1–35
☎ 03–2260251
🚋 11

Kleinblatt
Luxury Jewish pâtisserie, apple strudel in the winter and bilberry tarts in the summer.
✉ Provinciestraat 206
☎ 03–2337513
🚋 11

Kotee de Provence
Best of Provence: from olives to handmade lavender soap.
✉ St Jorispoort 11
☎ 03–2267183 🚋 8

Moeder Babelutte
Moeder Babelutte lived from 1841 to 1912 and invented the boiled sweet named after her in 1885. Other sweets on sale in this shop include hard and soft nougat, fruit and nut mix and humbugs.
✉ Hoogstraat 31 🚋 2, 15

Rarytas
Polish delicatessen for lovers of real sausage, duck pasty, gherkins and buckwheat pancakes for breakfast or lunch.
✉ Lange Leemstraat 109
🚋 8

Suikerjan
Family business producing handmade sweets. The son now runs the business.
✉ St Jacobsmarkt 42
☎ 03–2325788 🚋 11

Books, CDs & Records

Bilbo
Shop to browse in for almost unobtainable CDs at reduced prices.
✉ **Oude Koornmarkt 58**
☎ 03–2268480 🚊 2, 15

Blue Note from Ear & Eye
Trendy jazz shop with an enthusiastic owner who is happy to tell you about an old classic or a new discovery.
✉ **Oude Koornmarkt 53–58**
☎ 03–2264742 🚊 2, 15

FNAC
Branch of the French chain: sells books, CDs, games, electronic equipment and computers. Staff are very well trained and can give advice if you ask.
✉ **Groenplaats-GB Shoppingcenter** ☎ 03–2312056 🚊 2, 15

International Magazine Store
About 8,000 magazine titles on the shelves. You name it, there's a magazine about it and you can buy it here.
✉ **Melkmarkt 17**
☎ 03–2331668 🚊 11

Jenny Hannivers
English antiquarian bookseller. You can find rare works of English literature and the shop will also take your English books in part exchange.
✉ **Melkmarkt 30** ☎ **None**
🚊 11

De Markies
Remainder bookshop: slightly damaged books at 30 per cent off. Older remainders are even cheaper.
✉ **Melkmarkt 17**
☎ 03–2372437 🚊 11

Mekanik Strip
Strip cartoon shop with all the Belgian classics, American comics, a whole host of gadgets and an extensive selection of manga videos. The first floor has an exhibition of the work of strip cartoon writers, artists and cartoonists.
✉ **St Jacobsmarkt 73**
☎ 03–2342347 🚊 11

Metrophone
Wonderful place to browse for second-hand vinyl and CDs from the 1950s to the 1980s. You can spend hours searching in the bins for a nostalgic single from 1970.
✉ **Lange Koepoortstraat 70**
☎ 03–2525626
🚊 7

Schlock Entertainment
Videothèque specialising in horror movies and old cult films.
✉ **Diepestraat 104**
☎ 03–2267176
🚊 2

Standaard Boekhandel
A branch of one of the oldest bookshop chains in Flanders, which also stocks a fair range of English-language titles. If you haven't a copy of this travel guide go and buy it there.
✉ **Huidevettersstraat 57–59**
☎ 03–2310773 🚊 7

Taboo Records
Cutting-edge cult shop specialising in Goa-Trance, in Kammenstraat among the alternative clothing shops where you can find just the right outfit.
✉ **Kammenstraat 66**
☎ 03–2333973
🚊 2, 15

The Meir
The Meir is naturally *the* pedestrianised shopping street. It has all the big chains, for example Matinique. The Meir is also a lovely place to stroll, to see and be seen. There is always something to do: small street plays, mime, etc. Thousands of locals flock here on sunny Saturday afternoons.

Where to Take the Children

Child-friendly Antwerp

Antwerp is an extremely child-friendly city. In hotels and restaurants, as well as in museums, people have an eye to the interests of the young tourist. Many shops have a toy corner so that parents can shop in peace. The tourist office in Antwerp (03–2320103) can help you to find special attractions for the children.

Adventure Island

For youngsters from 12 to 18: laser shooting, table hockey, video games, the internet, bumper cars. Jungle parties, Star Trek parties and alien parties are organised in the summer.

✉ **Kribbestraat 11**
☎ **03–2252175** 🚊 **4, 7**

Circus

Children's fashion shop with brightly coloured shiny satin jackets, dresses and suits imported from Asia. There is second-hand clothing and also overstocks from top designers such as Paul Smith, Walter van Beirendonck and Dries van Noten. There is a section with children's books.

✉ **Kasteelpleinstraat 12**
☎ **03–2890332** 🚊 **7**

Dagbladmuseum

The history of the newspaper shown in pictures. There are also exhibitions for children about zoo animals, mills and the alphabet.

✉ **Lombardenvest 6**
☎ **03–2333299**
🚊 **2, 15**

Flandria cruise on the Schelt

A 50-minute cruise or a harbour cruise of two to three hours. Children always love it.

✉ **Scheldetocht: Steenplein Antwerpen; Havenrondvaart: Kaai 13–14 Londenbrug**
☎ **03–2313100** 🚊 **7**

Hortiflora

Gardens with a historic or modern theme. The Rubenstuin in particular appeals to the imagination (▶ 13).

✉ **Hoek Beukenlaan-Middelheimlaan** 🚌 **27, 32**

De Keiheuvel

Playground with play equipment in a giant sandpit with gangways, barrels, ropes, slides and lookout towers. There is also a swimming pool with a shallow pool for children and toddlers, and a trampoline park.

✉ **17e Esc. Lichtvliegwezenlaan 14, 2490 Balen** ☎ **014–810301**

Magic World

This is Antwerp in miniature. There is a sound and light presentation lasting about 20 minutes and you can visit the workshops and even the 'snail world'.

✉ **Cockerilkaai**
☎ **03–2370397** 🚊 **4**

Middelheim Openlucht-museum

Youngsters can come face to face with sculpture in a healthy open-air setting (▶ 54).

✉ **Middelheimlaan 61**
☎ **03–8281350** 🚌 **27, 32**

De Mosten

A pleasant family beach with fun in the water for all ages. There is also a playground, a miniature animal park, a lake for surfing or angling and other attractions.

✉ **Hoogeind 74, 2321 Hoog-straten** ☎ **03–3401951**

Nationaal Scheepvaartmuseum

In the old fortress the Steen (▶ 25), which in itself appeals to children. With a lovely collection of model ships. Outside there is harbour equipment to admire and a boat out of the water to visit.

✉ **Steenplein 1**
☎ **03–2320850** 🚊 **7**

Park Vogelenzang

Children can feed the deer and romp in the playground or on the playing fields (➤ 13).

📮 Gerard Le Grellelaan

🚋 27, 32

Pirateneiland

A former warehouse that has been converted into an indoor amusement park. Pirate's Island has all kinds of attractions for children from 2 to 12 years on several floors. Parents can join the children or enjoy a pizza in the cellar. There is a pirate club where children can be left supervised while parents go into town.

📮 Kribbestraat 12

☎ 03–2315813

🚋 4, 7

Planckendael

A lovely spacious park with many animals, the perfect supplement to Antwerp Zoo. As well as exotic animals there are many native ones that have all but disappeared in the wild.

📮 Leuvensesteenweg 582, 2812 Muizen (Mechelen)

☎ 015–414921

Stadspark (➤ 12)

The largest green lung in the centre of the city. It includes a large lake, a historic suspension bridge, smooth lawns, a playground (also suitable for the disabled). For sports fanatics there is a skateboard and roller-skate rink.

📮 Tegenover de van Eycklei

🚋 2, 15

St Annatunnel

Children love to walk through the pedestrian tunnel (500m) from the St Annaplein to the Linkeroever (➤ 66).

🚋 St Annaplein 🚋 4

Speelgoedmuseum (➤ 87)

Two floors with more than 30 sections. Children and grown-ups need not just look, they are also allowed to play with the toys.

📮 Nekkerspoel 21, 2800 Mechelen ☎ 015–557075

🚉 Near the Mechelen-Nekkerspoel Station

Speeltuin Kruisberg

Three-hectare playground with more than 50 items of equipment, including a wooden train and a spider's web. There is a separate play area for toddlers up to three years old.

📮 Wijngaard 4, 2200 Herentals

☎ 014–224224

Vleeshuis

Captures the imagination of youngsters, especially the collection of armour and harnesses. There is also an Egyptian section and a collection of old musical instruments.

📮 Vleeshouwersstraat 38–40

☎ 03–2336404

🚋 7

Volkskundemuseum

Children enjoy the puppets at the 'Poesje' theatre, the Giant and Giantess and the exhibition of conjuring tricks (➤ 112).

📮 Gildekamerstraat 2–6

☎ 03–2208653

🚋 2, 11, 15

Zoo

More than 6,000 animals and a playground (➤ 26).

📮 Koningin Astridplein 26

☎ 03–2024540

🚋 2, 15

Bobbejaanland

This family park is a paradise for children. It is an amusement park 30km from Antwerp. There is a special children's world where children from 2 years old are free to enjoy themselves. People are, of course, never too old for the real amusement park with rides such as the Looping, the Air Race and the Revolution.

📮 Steenweg op Olen 45, 2460 Lichtaart

☎ 014–557811

🕐 Apr–Oct: opening times vary

💷 Moderate

🚉 Special shuttle bus from Herentals Station

Classical Music & Theatre

Culture in Antwerp

Antwerp is an outstanding cultural city. Cultural events are organised throughout the year and there are, of course, always the many theatres and playhouses. Most theatre performances are in Dutch but the publication *Kalender Antwerpen* gives English renditions. Films are usually in the original language with Dutch sub-titles, but some are dubbed so be careful to check in advance.

There is a special cultural information desk and bookshop on the Grote Markt:

🖂 Grote Markt 40
☎ 03–2208111

Bourlaschouwburg

This used to be called the 'French Opera' to distinguish it from the 'Flemish Opera'. The renovated Bourla is now the home of the city theatre company the Toneelhuis (➤ 33).

🖂 **Komedieplaats 18**
☎ 03–2310750 🚊 7, 8

Culturele Infobalie

For all information on cultural events, plus bookshop.

🖂 **Grote Markt 40**
☎ 03–2208111
🚊 2, 15, 11

deSingel

Theatre complex with a modern outlook. There is also an annual multimedia event *De Nachten*.

🖂 **Desguinlei 25**
☎ 03–2482828 🚊 8

Echt Antwaarps Theater

Folk theatre company with typical local humour in the Antwerp dialect.

🖂 **Frans Beirenslaan 72**
☎ 03–3228700

Filharmonisch Huis

Home of the prestigious Koniklijk Filharmonisch Orkest (Royal Philharmonic Orchestra).

🖂 **Braziliëstraat 15**
☎ 03–2313737 🚊 4, 7

Hof ter Lo

Alternative concert hall for young people on the edge of the city.

🖂 **Noordersingel 30**
☎ 03–2350811
🚊 3, 12

Koningin Elisabethzaal

Concert hall in the heart of the city, near the zoo. Specialises in popular acts and light classical music.

🖂 Koningin Astridplein 23–24
☎ 03–2035600 🚊 2, 15

Koninklijk Ballet van Vlaanderen

Home of the Flemish ballet company.

🖂 **Kattendijkdok Westkaai 16**
☎ 03–2343438 🚊 4, 7

Koninklijke Poppenschouwburg van Campen

Theatre for high-quality puppets shows.

🖂 **Lange Nieuwstraat 3**
☎ 03–2373716 🚊 11

Het Paleis, Stadsschouwburg

The successor to the Koninklijk Jeugdtheater (Royal Youth Theatre). The Paleis often works with 'adult' theatres which can only be a positive benefit.

🖂 Meistraat 2 ☎ 03–2028360
🚊 2, 15

Poesje

Lively puppet theatre near the Vleeshuis.

🖂 Repenstraat ☎ 03–2329409
🚊 2, 11, 15

Stadsschouwburg

City theatre complex on the edge of the Wapper.

🖂 **Theaterplein 1**
☎ 03–2270306 🚊 2, 15

Vlaamse Opera

Flemish Opera House with an internationally renowned programme.

🖂 **Frankrijklei 3**
☎ 03–2336808 🚊 11

Zuiderpershuis

World cultural centre in a beautifully renovated building (➤ 70).

🖂 **Waalse Kaai 14**
☎ 03–2487077 🚊 4, 8

Live Music

Café Modern
Trendy young people's café with live performances on Thursdays and DJs at the weekend. Close to the pedestrian tunnel.
✉ St Jansvliet 10 🚊 4

Crossroads
For lovers of Blue Grass and Tex Mex. Live music on Sunday afternoons. Popular with students and schoolchildren during the week.
✉ Mechelsesteenweg 8
☎ 03–2315266
🚊 7, 8

Elephants Graveyard
Irish café with a great reputation. At the weekend there are concerts by (as yet) unknown groups who give Irish pop or Belgian-Irish blues their best.
✉ Drukkerijstraat 1
☎ 03–2250274
🚊 2, 15

Hopper
Popular jazz café on the Museumplein, for a lazy afternoon and evening.
✉ Leopold de Waelstraat 2
☎ 03–2484933
🚊 4, 8

Kaffee 10/10
Soul and jazz bar in the disctrict of Antwerp North. Live music every Thursday evening.
✉ St Elisabethstraat 38
☎ 03–2355553

Kids Rhythm'n'Blues Danskaffee
Swinging disco on the Grote Market with a free concert every Sunday.
✉ Grote Markt 50
☎ 03–2273585
🚊 2, 11, 15

Muziekdoos
Trendy but far too small folk café. Free stage for jazz musicians on Wednesdays, and for singers and songwriters on Thursdays.
✉ Verschansingstraat 63
🚊 4

Refrein
Popular music café with live music on Thursdays and Sundays, from Irish folk and French *chansons* to jazz and Cuban music.
✉ Pelgrimstraat 11
☎ 03–2311689
🚊 2, 11, 15

De Muze
Jazz and artists' café with roots in the 1960s. Live music almost every evening. All the big names in Antwerp began here.
✉ Melkmarkt 15
☎ 03–2260126 🚊 11

Royal Cirque Belge
Yuppie haunt with the better end of Belgian pop live on Thursday, Friday and Saturday evenings. The food is excellent.
✉ Groenplaats 34–35
☎ 03–2329439
🚊 2, 15

Scene
Rave bar for students and music lovers, with live techno or grunge on Wednesday evenings.
✉ Graaf van Hoornestraat 2
☎ 03–2386462
🚊 4, 8

Teranga
Hot Senegalese dance café with live music on Thursdays, Fridays and Saturdays.
✉ Van Stralenstraat 6
🚊 11

Live Music in Antwerp
Antwerp nightlife encourages music. Where once De Muze café set the trend there are now more and more pubs where, in exchange for a drink and some small change from the customers, the management is happy to give young talent the (small) stage – which can only add to the atmosphere.

Discos

Nightlife in Antwerp
Nightlife in Antwerp is among the most vibrant in Flanders. There is no official closing time. When one disco finishes another is opening for an '*après* party'. Antwerp is a place where you can go out for the whole night, right through until the early afternoon of the following day.

Le Beau Zoo
Cosmopolitan disco for young professionals who like to drink champagne on the dance floor.
- St Godefriduskaai 50
- 03–2131400
- 4, 7

Café Local
Sultry dance café for lovers of salsa and merengue music.
- Waalse Kaai 25
- 03–2385004 4, 8

Exodus
'*Après* club' to recover after a heavy night out.
- Van Schoonhovenstraat 24
- 2, 11, 15

Café d'Anvers
Modern cult disco in the heart of the red light district of Antwerp.
- Verversrui 15
- 03–2263870
- 4, 7

The Phil Collins Club
Techno disco with lively DJ. The owners organise the 'I love Techno' festival.
- Lange Schipperskapelstraat 11–13 03–2324712
- 4, 7

Flavers
Home of hip-hop and soul in Antwerp. Friday evening is Ladies' Night.
- Anneessensstraat
- 2, 11, 15

Kafe Marque
New-wave disco appropriately in a cellar, for lovers of gothic and grunge and the darker music of the 1980s.
- Grote Pieter Potstraat 3
- 03–2332428
- 11

New Editions
Trendy soul café. The public has dressed up to go out, the DJs rap and scratch. A place to have a vodka before you dance.
- Breydelstraat 25
- 2, 15

Red & Blue
Popular gay café with a house rule that refuses women entry. They have the smartest toilet attendant in Antwerp.
- Lange Schipperskapelstraat 11–13 03–2130555
- 4, 7

River Club
Trendy disco for champagne parties to funky rhythm or the hits of the 1980s.
- Luikstraat 6 03–2373978
- 4, 8

Space (Obeliks)
Trendy '*après* club' for those who don't want to or can't go home on Sunday morning. Trance music until late on Sunday afternoon.
- Frankrijklei 29 2

Tangofabriek El Sur
Those who want to go out and find salsa and merengue too easy. Tangofabriek also gives lessons in tango. Shiny shoes are a must.
- Hertdeinstraat 29
- 03–2326720
- 2, 15

Zillion
Mega disco with four halls, each with different decor and music, a giant aquarium, a moving dance floor, and much more.
- Jan van Gentstraat 4
- 03–2481516
- 4, 8

Bars & Café-Bars

Bar Tabac
Night-time bar with an international reputation. Jungle, jazz, acid jazz and trip–hop music.
✉ **Waalse Kaai 43**
🚊 4, 8

Bato Batu
Traditional bar with a plain interior that stays open until early morning.
✉ **St Jorispoort 1**
☎ 03–2340319 🚊 7, 8

Den Artist
Romantic wine bar right opposite the Museum voor Schone Kunsten that claims to have more than 10,000 bottles of wine in the cellar.
✉ **Museumstraat 46**
☎ 03–2380995 🚊 4, 7

Den Bengel
Very attractive traditional bar on the Grote Markt. The terrace is popular with tourists in the summer.
✉ **Grote Markt 5**
☎ 03–2333290
🚊 2, 11, 15

Celtic Ireland
Irish bar serving food with an abundance of atmosphere and naturally plenty of draught stout.
✉ **Groenplaats 1**
☎ 03–2131450 🚊 2, 15

Entrepot du Congo
Trendy artists' café well known for the 30 types of whisky on its list.
✉ **Vlaamse Kaai 42**
☎ 03–2389232
🚊 4, 8

Gounod
Bar close to the Bourlaschouwburg. During performances it is not unknown to spot actors in full costume having a swift drink.
✉ **Kelderstraat 4**
☎ 03–2263943
🚊 7, 8

Koetshuis
Culture café in the former coach house of Jacob Jordaens's house.
✉ **Reyndersstraat 6**
☎ 03–2010013
🚊 2, 11, 15

De Plansjee
Alternative music café with a bar atmosphere, on the corner of the beautiful Hendrik Conscienceplein.
✉ **Hoek Wolstraat-Conscienceplein**
☎ 03–2260944
🚊 11

Popi
Pleasant café with a welcome. *Popi* is Russian for 'backside'.
✉ **Riemstraat 22**
☎ 03–2381530
🚊 4, 8

De Soete Naem Jesus
Sultry Afro-Caribbean café.
✉ **Oude Koornmarkt 40**
☎ 03–2337179 🚊 2, 15

TV1 Café
Theme bar with the stars of the VRT channel. Fans can have a pint in the hope of seeing a famous Fleming.
✉ **Grote Markt 1**
🚊 2, 11, 15

Vagant
Bar specialising in gin that has more than 100 different varieties on offer, both Belgian and Dutch.
✉ **Reyndersstraat 25**
☎ 03–2331538
🚊 2, 11, 15

Bars in Antwerp
There are more than 1,800 bars and café-bars of all kinds in Antwerp. Most of them have at least two kinds of draught beer and also offer an extensive selection of bottled beers. If you cannot make up your mind, ask the barman for advice. He will be happy to recommend a good beer.

What's On When

Opening of the Tourist Season
Every year, a week before or a week after Easter, the tourist season opens officially in Antwerp with a wealth of events. There is a different theme each year but whatever it is it guarantees a weekend in the city full of atmosphere and sensation.

January/February
The winter sales starts at the beginning of January; Chinese New Year parades in and around van Wesebekestraat (➤ 67); promenade concert in the Elisabethzaal; 16-day cycling event on the track in the Sportpaleis; Europalia exhibition in Museum voor Fotografie (➤ 54); international water polo tournament.

March/April
International carnival procession in Ekeren; annual pilgrims' meal in the chapel of St Julianusgasthuis; European youth film festival; indoor Caribbean festival 'Antillean celebrations' in the Sportpaleis; Erotica market in the Sportpaleis; open studios in Antwerp Central where artists display their work; cross-country championships in Deurne; Antwerp marathon; official opening of the tourist season in Antwerp.

May
May Day processions and speeches; VE Day anniversary 8 May; park day; 'Grand Prix of Europe' powerboat race on the Scheldt; music festival in Groenplaats and the Zoo; start of carillon concerts; festival markets in Antwerp and Wilrijk.

June
Carillon concerts; international music festival in Ekeren; environment fair; festival market in Deurne; Whitsun fair on the former Zuiderdokken; cycle race for amateurs *Rerum Novarum*.

July
Mussel festival; festival of the Flemish community; national day; carpet of flowers on the Grote Markt; carillon concerts; Summer in Antwerp events; jazz in Grote Markt; concerts in Antwerp Cathedral; world folklore festival in Schoten; rhythm 'n' blues festival.

August
Antwerp guild festivals; Flanders cultural market; jazz on the Hei; Rubens market.

September
Seniors' month in the Zoo; liberation celebrations; homage to the dead in Deurne; fireworks in Deurne; Kloosterstraat festivals; monuments open day; giant parade in Borgerhout; Antwerp boat show; industry open day; September fair in Ekeren; Cluysekermis (fair); street run in Deurne; Antwerp Ten Miles and Ladies Five Match; international amateur cycle race.

October/November
Train-tram-bus day; 24 hours of special Belgian beers; come-for-a-walk day; antique dealers' open days; Night of the Proms in the Sportpaleis; Flemish book fair.

December
Setting up the Christmas tree; switching on the tree lights; Sunday shopping; Antwerp goes skating; journey to the crib; Night of the Proms in the Sportpaleis; New Year fireworks.

Practical Matters

Above: *a police van*

Right: *a map of the city and a board showing the tram timetable*

TIME DIFFERENCES

GMT
12 noon

Belgium
1PM

British Summer
1PM

Netherlands
1PM

USA (NY)
7AM

USA (LA)
4AM

BEFORE YOU GO

WHAT YOU NEED

		Belgium	Netherlands	Germany	UK	USA
●	Required					
○	Suggested					
▲	Not required					
Passport/National Identity Card		●	●	●	●	●
Visa		▲	▲	▲	▲	▲
Onward or Return Ticket		▲	○	○	○	○
Health Inoculations		▲	▲	▲	▲	▲
Health Documentation (► Health, 123)		▲	●	●	●	●
Travel Insurance		○	○	○	○	○
Driving Licence (national)		●	●	●	●	●
Green Card (if own car)		▲	●	●	●	●
Car Registration Document (if own car)		▲	●	●	●	●

WHEN TO GO

Antwerp

High season

Low season

5°C	6°C	9°C	11°C	15°C	18°C	20°C	20°C	19°C	15°C	10°C	6°C
JAN	FEB	MAR	APR	MAY	JUN	JUL	AUG	SEP	OCT	NOV	DEC

Very wet Wet Cloudy Sun Sun/showers

TOURIST OFFICES

In the UK
Belgian Tourist Office
29 Princes Street
London W1R 7RG
☎ 0900 188 7799

In the USA
Suite 1501
780 Third Avenue
New York NY 10017
☎ 212/758-8130

In Belgium
Toerisme Vlaanderen
Grasmarkt 63
1000 Brussel
☎ 02–5040390

POLICE 101

FIRE 100

AMBULANCE 100

WHEN YOU ARE THERE

ARRIVING

Antwerp is 50km from the international airport at Zaventem and has its own commercial airport in Deurne. The Centraal Station means Antwerp is easily accessible by rail from all major European cities. British visitors can take Eurostar to Brussels, then a short train journey (35 min.) to Antwerp.

Zaventem Airport kilometres to city centre	**Journey times**	
	🚋	40 minutes
50km	🚌	30 minutes
	🚗	30 minutes

Antwerp Centraal Station in the city centre	**Journey times**	
	🚋	available
	🚌	available
	🚗	available

TIME

 Belgium follows Central European Time (CET) which is one hour ahead of Greenwich Mean Time (GMT+1), but from the end of March to the end of October it is on summertime (GMT+2).

CUSTOMS

 YES

From a non-EU country for personal use:
Cigarettes: 200 or
Tobacco: 250 grams
Spirits : 1 litre or
Fortified wine (sherry, port): 2 litres
Wine: 2 litres

From an EU country for personal use (guidelines):
Cigarettes: 800 or
Tobacco: 1 kilogram
Spirits: 10 litres or
Fortified wine: 20 litres
Wine: 90 litres
Beer: 110 litres

 NO

Drugs, firearms, explosives, offensive weapons, protected animal species.

MONEY

The unit of currency is the euro but until December 2001, the Belgian franc will continue to be used. A dual pricing system will operate. In January 2002 euro bank notes and coins will replace the Belgian franc which will cease to be legal tender in July 2002. Euro notes come in denominations of 10, 20, 50, 100, 200 and 500 and coins in denominations of 1, 2, 5,10, 20 and 50 centimes, 1 and 2 euros.

EMBASSIES (IN BRUSSELS)

UK
02–2876211

USA
02–5082111

Australia
02–2310500

Canada
02–7410611

WHEN YOU ARE THERE

TOURIST OFFICES

Tourist information
The tourist office, **Toerisme Antwerpen**, can provide information about Antwerp, including what to see, events, cultural activities, restaurants and accommodation. You can also make hotel reservations or book a city guided tour.

Tourist information for the Province of Antwerp is provided by a separate office, **Toerisme Provincie Antwerpen**. **VSW Prospekta** has information on cultural events: theatre, ballet and so on and you can also buy tickets.

Finally in the **Stadswinkel**, the city information office, you can find answers to questions from 'Living in Antwerp' to 'My car has been towed away, how do I get it back?' Locals often make use of it.

Toerisme Antwerpen
● Grote Markt 15
 B-2000 Antwerpen
 ☎ 03-2320103

Toerisme Provincie Antwerpen
● Koningin Elisabethlei 16
 2018 Antwerpen
 ☎ 03-2406373

VZW Prospekta
● Grote Markt 40
 B-2000 Antwerpen
 ☎ 03-2208111

Stadswinkel
● Grote Markt 40
 B-2000 Antwerpen
 ☎ 03-2208180

NATIONAL HOLIDAYS

J	F	M	A	M	J	J	A	S	O	N	D
1		(1)	(1)	1	(3)	(1)	(2)	2	1	1	2

1 Jan	New Year's Day
Mar/Apr	Easter Monday
May	1 May, May Day
May/Jun	Ascension Day
May/Jun	Whit Monday
11 Jul	Flemish National Day
21 Jul	Belgian National Day
15 Aug	Assumption
27 Sep	Walloon National Day
1 Nov	All Saints' Day
11 Nov	Armistice Day
25 Dec	Christmas Day

Most shops, banks and offices are closed on these days. The Flemish and Walloon National Days are not official holidays but they are generally celebrated.

OPENING TIMES

○ Shops	● Post Offices
● Offices	● Museums
● Banks	● Pharmacies

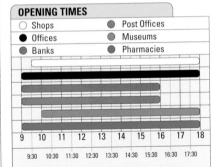

9   10   11   12   13   14   15   16   17   18

9:30   10:30   11:30   12:30   13:30   14:30   15:30   16:30   17:30

Some shops close in the afternoon. Other shops are open on Saturday but are closed on Monday. In Antwerp you will find a number of shops that are open beyond normal hours until 1 or 2AM or even all night. Pharmacies have a night and weekend rota which is displayed on the door of all pharmacies when they are closed. You can also ask the tourist office for the duty pharmacist (03–2320103).

The opening times for museums vary enormously, ask at the individual museum. Most are closed on Monday.

DRIVE ON THE RIGHT

TOILETS NOT FREE

PUBLIC TRANSPORT

 Metro The metro is the fastest form of transport in Antwerp, especially as parking can be a problem in the centre of the city. The network serves the whole city centre. Metro trains are clean, safe and relatively cheap. If you are making several journeys it is worth asking about a day pass or a ten-journey ticket, which can also be used on the buses and trams.

 Train Trains connect Antwerp with the rest of Belgium and are relatively cheap. There are direct connections to all the big cities (Brussels, Ghent, Mechelen) and you can travel almost anywhere in Belgium by a combination of train and bus.

 Bus The bus is the recommended means of transport within Greater Antwerp to places that are not covered by the metro network. The bus is less practical than the metro/tram in the city centre because journeys are slower.

CAR RENTAL

 There are many car rental firms offering competitive prices. The major firms have free phone numbers (0800–), and you can find the numbers and details in *De Gouden Gids* (*Yellow Pages*). Expect to pay extra for unlimited mileage but not for insurance. There are weekend rates everywhere. You must be at least 21 and hold a valid European or international driving licence. Most firms insist on payment by credit card, or will require a hefty cash deposit.

TAXIS

 There are many taxi ranks in the city. In addition, in cafés and restaurants you can ask for a taxi to be ordered, and there is usually no charge for this service. Every taxi has a meter that displays the actual amount to be paid plus any night supplement. Taxi drivers appreciate a small tip of 5–10 per cent that rounds up the fare. Journeys within Antwerp cost about 8–15 euros (BF300–600).

DRIVING

 Maximum speed limits on motorways: **120 kph.** Mimimum: **90 kph** unless otherwise stated. Speed limit in 'zone 30' streets: **30 kph.**

 Speed limit on all main roads: **90 kph.**

 Speed limit in built-up areas: **50 kph.**

 Front and rear seat belts are mandatory.

 Blood alcohol limit 0.5%. Random breath tests are made regularly.

 Petrol is sold by the litre in Belgium. Filling stations have standard 98 octane unleaded petrol, 95 octane unleaded petrol, lead-substitute and diesel. Most filling stations are self-service and accept credit cards.

 Driving in Antwerp itself is not recommended. Parking is difficult to find and expensive. If you have an accident with a rental car phone the rental company or the emergency number on the rental agreement.

SAFETY

Antwerp is a relatively safe place but beware of pickpockets and confidence tricksters in the tourist areas.

- Take care of your handbag and possessions, particularly in tourist areas and on the tram/metro.
- Do not leave any valuables visible in the car.
- Take with you only the amount of money that you will need. Leave passports, tickets, valuables and copies of your documents in the hotel safe.
- Report theft or mugging to the nearest police station; you will be given a record for your insurance company.

Police assistance:
☎ **101**

TELEPHONES

There are telephones on many street corners. Most take phone cards that are on sale in newsagents. International calls always begin with 00.

International Dialling Codes	
From Belgium to:	
UK:	**00 44**
Ireland:	**00 353**
USA/Canada:	**00 1**
Australia:	**00 61**
Netherlands:	**00 31**
Germany:	**00 49**

POST

Post Offices
The main Post Office is at Groenplaats 43 A1 and this office is also open on Saturday afternoon. There are also post offices in various places throughout the city and post boxes on street corners in most neighbourhoods.

ELECTRICITY

In Belgium the power supply is 220 volts AC. Plugs are round with two pins. British

appliances will need an adaptor. For most non-European equipment you will also need a transformer to 100–120 volts AC.

TIPS/GRATUITIES

Yes ✓ No ✗		
Restaurants	✗	
Hotels (chambermaids, porters)	✗	
Bars	✗	
Doormen in discos	✓	
Taxis	✗	
Guides	✓	
Cloakroom attendants	✓	
Toilets	✓	
Hairdressers	✓	

PHOTOGRAPHY

What to photograph: From the Brabo Fountain on the Grote Markt to animals in the zoo. The Antwerp skyline is beautiful, especially in the evening from the left bank.

Where to photograph: Photography not allowed in some public buildings and churches. It is sensible to ask permission before you photograph people.

Where to buy film: chemists, supermarkets, camera shops, etc.

HEALTH

Insurance

Within the EU there are agreements about the payment of medical costs for visitors from other member states, but not all risks are covered. For example, you will need extra insurance to cover dental treatment. Ask your travel insurer what cover you need for Belgium. Some credit cards provide insurance cover if you book your holiday with a card, but it is unwise to rely on this for full cover. Non-EU visitors need full medical cover.

Dentist

Make sure that your medical insurance covers dental treatment.

Sun Advice

It is rarely hot in Antwerp. If it is use sun cream and drink plenty of fluids.

Drugs

There is a pharmacy on every corner that will dispense prescriptions or provide over-the-counter remedies. If you need regular medication take it with you plus the prescription (for customs). There is a weekend and night rota for pharmacists and doctors in Antwerp. The duty pharmacists are listed on the door of the pharmacies that are closed. You can also obtain this information from the tourist office (03–2320103).

Safe Water

You can safely drink the tap water. Mineral water is cheap and easily obtainable. If you ask for a glass of water in a café or restaurant, you will be served mineral water and be expected to pay for it.

CONCESSIONS

Students/young people There are student concessions at many attractions on production of student card or proof of age.

Senior citizens Discounts are available for senior citizens at many attractions. You need to be over 65. Some restaurants also give a reduction, ask about it.

CLOTHING SIZES

UK	USA	Belgium /Europe	
36	36	46	
38	38	48	
40	40	50	Suits
42	42	52	
44	44	54	
46	46	56	
7	8	41	
7.5	8.5	42	
8.5	9.5	43	Shoes
9.5	10.5	44	
10.5	11.5	45	
11	12	46	
14.5	14.5	37	
15	15	38	
15.5	15.5	39/40	Shirts
16	16	41	
16.5	16.5	42	
17	17	43	
8	6	34	
10	8	36	
12	10	38	Dresses
14	12	40	
16	14	42	
18	16	44	
4.5	6	38	
5	6.5	38	
5.5	7	39	Shoes
6	7.5	39	
6.5	8	40	
7	8.5	41	

WHEN DEPARTING

- Phone the airport, allow plenty of time and make sure you arrive at the check in at least two hours before departure.
- A taxi is the quickest way to get to the airport at Deurne, for Zaventem it is better to go by train.
- Airport tax is included in your ticket.

LANGUAGE

Dutch is the official language of Flanders. Most young inhabitants of Antwerp also speak English, whilst the older ones speak French. The Antwerp dialect itself is alive and kicking, although tourists are not expected to speak it.

Not everybody speaks English, though, making it useful to know some Dutch words, and attempts to use them will be appreciated. The 'oo' (pronounced 'oa' as in load) and 'ee' constructions (pronounced 'ay' as in day) are particularly problematic for English-speakers. If you pronounce 'ij' like English 'eye' you'll be close enough: for example *prijs* 'price'; *ontbijt* 'ontbite'.

hotel	*hotel*	breakfast	*ontbijt*
room	*kamer*	toilet	*toilet/WC*
single/	*eenpersoonskamer/*	bathroom	*badkamer*
double	*tweepersoonskamer*	shower	*douche*
one/two nights	*een/twee nachten*	balcony	*balkon*
per person/	*per persoon/*	key	*sleutel*
per room	*per kamer*	room service	*room service*
reservation	*reservering*	chambermaid	*kamermeisje*
rate	*prijs*		

bank	*bank*	American dollar	*Amerikaanse dollar*
exchange office	*wisselkantoor*	banknote	*papiergeld*
post office	*postkantoor*	coin	*wisselgeld/kleingeld*
cashier	*kassa*	credit card	*creditcard*
foreign exchange	*buitenlands geld*	traveller's cheque	*reisecheque*
currency	*valuta*	exchange rate	*wisselkoers*
British pound	*Engels/Britse pond*	commission charge	*commissie*

restaurant	*restaurant*	starter	*voorgerecht*
café	*café*	main course	*hoofdgerecht*
table	*tafel*	dish of the day	*dagschotel*
menu	*menukaart*	dessert	*nagerecht*
set menu	*menu*	drink	*drank/drankje*
wine list	*wijnkaart*	waiter	*ober*
lunch	*lunch/middageten*	waitress	*serveerster*
dinner	*diner/avondeten*	the bill	*de rekening*

aeroplane	*vliegtuig*	single/return	*enkele reis/retour*
airport	*luchthaven*	first/	*eerste klas/*
train	*trein*	second class	*tweede klas*
station	*station*	ticket office	*boekingskantoor*
bus	*bus*	timetable	*dienstregeling*
station	*busstation*	seat	*plaats*
ferry	*veerboot*	non-smoking	*niet roken*
port	*haven*	reserved	*gereserveerd*
ticket	*reisekaart*	taxi!	*taxi!*

yes	*ja*	help!	*help!*
no	*nee*	today	*vandaag*
please	*alstublieft*	tomorrow	*morgen*
thank you	*dank u*	yesterday	*gisteren*
hello	*dag/hallo*	how much?	*hoeveel?*
goodbye	*dag/tot ziens*	expensive	*duur*
goodnight	*welterusten*	closed	*gesloten*
sorry	*excuseer/pardon*	open	*geopend*

Acknowledgements
The publishers would like to thank the following photographers and libraries for their assistance in the preparation of this book:

ARCHIEF EN MUSEUM VOOR HET VLAAMSE CULTUURLEVEN ANTWERPEN – PHOTOGRAPHER: BART HUYSMANS 32, BELGACOM 122a, DIAMANTMUSEUM ANTWERPEN 20, DIENST VOOR TOERISME ANTWERPEN 9a, DIENST VOOR TOERISME GEEL – 1997: G. CHARLIER 75, 76, DIENST VOOR TOERISME HOOGSTRATEN 73, 78, DIENST VOOR TOERISME LIER 80, 83, DIENST VOOR TOERISME TURNHOUT 90, ETNOGRAFISCH MUSEUM ANTWERPEN – PHOTOGRAPHER: HUGHES DUBOIS 39a, JEROEN VAN DER SPEK 21, MUSEUM PLANTIN – MORETUS / STEDELIJK PRENTENKABINET – PHOTOGRAPHER: PETER MAES 10, 22, MUSEUM VOOR FOTOGRAFIE ANTWERPEN 54, POLITIE ANTWERPEN 122b, TEO VAN GERWEN DESIGN 5b, 8, 15a, 15b, 17, 23, 27b, 28, 35, 36, 37, 38, 39b, 40, 41, 42, 44, 45, 46, 47, 49, 50, 51, 52, 53, 56a, 56b, 57a, 57b, 58, 59, 61, 62, 63, 64b, 65, 66, 67, 69, 70, 71, 72, 77, 79, 81, 82, 84, 85, 88, 89, 91a, 91b, 117a, 117b, 122c, TOERISME ANTWERPEN 1, 2 5a, 6, 7, 11, 12, 13, 16, 18, 19, 24, 25, 27a, 29, 33, 34, 61, 57b, 60, 64a, 68, **TOERISME VLAANDEREN**: A. KOUPRIANOFF, D. DE KIEVITH 26, H.L. WEICHSELBAUM 86, M. DECLEER 48, TOERISME VLAANDEREN 9b, 14, 87

Dear Essential Traveller

Your comments, opinions and recommendations are very important to us. So please help us to improve our travel guides by taking a few minutes to complete this simple questionnaire.

You do not need a stamp (unless posted outside the UK). If you do not want to cut this page from your guide, then photocopy it or write your answers on a plain sheet of paper.

Send to: **The Editor, AA World Travel Guides,
FREEPOST SCE 4598, Basingstoke RG21 4GY.**

Your recommendations...

We always encourage readers' recommendations for restaurants, nightlife or shopping – if your recommendation is used in the next edition of the guide, we will send you a *FREE* AA *Essential* **Guide** of your choice. Please state below the establishment name, location and your reasons for recommending it.

_____

_____

_____

_____

Please send me **AA *Essential*** _____

(see list of titles inside the front cover)

About this guide...

Which title did you buy?
   AA *Essential* _____
Where did you buy it? _____
When? m m / y y

Why did you choose an AA *Essential* Guide? _____

_____

_____

_____

_____

Did this guide meet your expectations?
   Exceeded ☐   Met all ☐   Met most ☐   Fell below ☐
   Please give your reasons_____

_____

_____

_____

continued on next page...

Were there any aspects of this guide that you particularly liked? _____

_____

_____

_____

Is there anything we could have done better? _____

_____

_____

_____

_____

About you...

Name (*Mr/Mrs/Ms*) _____

    Address _____

_____

_____ Postcode _____

    Daytime tel nos _____

Which age group are you in?
    Under 25 ☐ 25–34 ☐ 35–44 ☐ 45–54 ☐ 55–64 ☐ 65+ ☐

How many trips do you make a year?
    Less than one ☐ One ☐ Two ☐ Three or more ☐

Are you an AA member? Yes ☐ No ☐

About your trip...

When did you book? m m / y y   When did you travel? m m / y y
How long did you stay? _____
Was it for business or leisure? _____
Did you buy any other travel guides for your trip?
    If yes, which ones? _____

_____

Thank you for taking the time to complete this questionnaire. Please send
    it to us as soon as possible, and remember, you do not need a stamp
    (*unless posted outside the UK*).

Happy Holidays!